ERNST TOLLER

Born in 1893, Toller volunteered for service in the First World War, was wounded and invalided out in 1916. He studied at university before getting caught up in the revolutionary activity that swept Germany following her defeat in 1918. He played an active role in the November Revolution in Munich, becoming Chairman of the briefly victorious Independent Socialist Party, but was arrested in June 1919, tried for treason and, at the age of 25, sentenced to five years in prison. It was there that he became a writer. Most of his best poetry and all four major plays were written in jail: *Transfiguration*, *Masses and Man*, *The Machine Wreckers* and *Hinkemann*. After his release in 1924, he travelled widely as a political speaker and writer. He fled Germany after the Reichstag fire in 1933: the Nazis burnt his books, black-listed him and stripped him of his citizenship. He lived in England on and off for two years, still politically and theatrically active, before moving to the United States. He committed suicide in New York at the age of 45, shortly before the outbreak of the Second World War.

A Selection of Other Volumes in this Series

*Published by Theatre Communications Group, distributed by Nick Hern Books

ERNST TOLLER

THE MACHINE WRECKERS

English version by
Ashley Dukes

ROYAL NATIONAL THEATRE
London

NICK HERN BOOKS
London

A Nick Hern Book

The Machine Wreckers first published in this edition
in Great Britain in 1995 as a paperback original
jointly by the Royal National Theatre, London, and
Nick Hern Books Limited, 14 Larden Road, London W3 7ST
by arrangement with A & C Black (Publishers) Limited

Die Maschinenstürmer was first published by E.P. Tal,
Leipzig, in 1922. Ashley Dukes's English version,
The Machine-Wreckers, was first published
by Benn Brothers, London, in 1923

Front cover: detail from 'March of the Weavers'
by Käthe Kollwitz (Philadelphia Museum of Art)

Typeset by Country Setting, Woodchurch, Kent TN26 3TB
Printed and bound in Great Britain by Cox & Wyman Ltd,
Reading, Berkshire

A CIP catalogue record for this book is available
from the British Library

ISBN 1 85459 288 2

Ernst Toller: a Brief Chronology

1893   1 Dec: Born in Samotschin near Bromberg.

1914   Aug: **Outbreak of First World War.** Volunteers for military service, thirteen months on Western Front.

1916   May-1917 Dec: Discharged on grounds of ill health. Hospitalised, then studies at Munich and Heidelberg Universities.

1918   Jan: Takes part in munition workers' strike in Munich. Nov: **Sailors' Mutiny in Kiel. Revolution in Berlin. Kaiser flees. Ebert (Social Democrat) emerges as leader. Armistice signed.** Toller plays leading part in short-lived Bavarian Revolution (Nov-1919 May).

1919   Jan: **Spartacist uprising in Berlin: leaders Karl Liebknecht and Rosa Luxemburg shot. Elections held for national assembly of ' Weimar Republic'.** 6 June: Toller arrested on charge of treason. 28 June: **Treaty of Versailles signed.** 14-16 July: Toller tried and sentenced to five years' imprisonment. 30 Sept: premiere of first play, *Die Wandlung (Transfiguration)*, in Berlin.

1920   March: **Unsuccessful right-wing Kapp putsch in Berlin.** 15 April: Premiere of play *Masse-Mensch (Masses and Man)* in Nuremburg.

1921   Publication of *Gedichte der Gefangenen (Prisoners' Poems)*, poems. 29 Sept: *Masses and Man* opens in Berlin.

1922   30 June: premiere of play *Die Maschinenstürmer (The Machine Wreckers)* in Berlin.

1923   Jan: **Occupation of the Ruhr by French troops.** 19 Sept: Premiere of play *Hinkemann* in Leipzig. Oct: **Unsuccessful Communist uprisings in Saxony and Hamburg.** 8-9 Nov: **Hitler's unsuccessful Munich beer-hall putsch.** 20 Nov: **the German mark falls to 4,200,000,000 to the dollar.**

1924   Publication of *Das Swalbenbuch (The Swallow Book)* and *Vormorgen (Before Morning)*, poems. 17 Jan: Riot at Dresden opening of *Hinkemann*. 15 July: Toller released from prison and expelled from Bavaria. Aug: **Dawes Plan for easing payment of war reparations implemented. The new Reichsmark introduced.** 2-6 Aug: Toller is guest of honour at Arbeiter-Kulturwoche (Trades Unions' Cultural Festival) in Leipzig. 16 Nov: Premiere of play

Der Entfesselte Wotan (Woden Unbound) in Moscow. Dec: Tour of Czechoslovakia.

1925   Feb: **Ebert dies. Hindenburg elected President.** March: Tour of Near East and Palestine. 8 Nov: Toller delivers speech entitled *Deutsche Revolution* to Berlin workers in Grosses Schauspielhaus.

1926   Jan: Brief trip to London. March-May: First visit to Soviet Union.

1927   Publication of *Justiz*, essays, documents etc., on theme of justice. March: Tour of Scandinavia. 1 and 3 Sept: Premiere of play *Hoppla, wir leben! (Hoppla! Such is Life!)* in Hamburg and Berlin.

1928   Spring: Brief trip to London.

1929   2 Feb: Premiere of play *Bourgeois bleibt Bourgeois (Once a Bourgeois, Always a Bourgeois)* in Berlin. Sept-Dec: First visit to United States (and Mexico). Oct: **Stresemann dies. Wall Street crashes.**

1930   Publication of *Quer Durch,* essays, and *Verbruderung,* selected writings. 31 Aug: Premiere of play *Feuer aus den Kesseln (Draw the Fires!)* in Berlin. 1 Sept: **The Young Plan for reparations implemented.** 14 Sept: **Elections show sensational rises in Communist and Nazi votes.** 17 Oct: Premiere of play *Wunder in Amerika (Mary Baker Eddy,* later called *Miracle in America)* in Mannheim.

1932   Spring: Tour through Republican Spain. **Unemployment in Germany tops 6,000,000. Hitler outvoted by Hindenburg in presidential election.** July: **Elections give Nazis 230 Reichstag seats.** 31 Oct: premiere of play *Die Blinde Göttin (The Blind Goddess)* in Vienna.

1933   30 Jan: **Hitler becomes Chancellor of Germany.** 27 Feb: **Reichstag Fire.** Toller leaves Germany for ever: goes to Switzerland then to England, where he is based until 1936. 10 May: **Nazi book burning, including Toller's.** 23 Aug: Toller black-listed by Nazis and deprived of German citizenship. Autumn: Publication of *Eine Jugend in Deutschland (I Was a German),* autobiography.

1934   Aug-Oct: Second visit to Soviet Union. Attends First Congress of Soviet Writers in Leningrad.

1935   Publication of *Briefe aus dem Gefängnis (Letters from Prison).* 10 Feb: Toller co-directs *Draw the Fires!* in Manchester (and later in London). March: Marries actress Christine Grautoff.

1936   11 June: Premiere of play *Nie Wieder Friede (No More Peace!)* in London. July: outbreak of Spanish Civil War.

12 Oct-1937 Feb: Second tour of United States (and Canada), lecturing chiefly on dangers of fascism.

1937   Spring-1938 Spring: Mostly in Santa Monica, California, working on film scripts for MGM.

1938   12 March: **German troops march into Austria.** July-Sept: Trip to war-torn Spain. Sept-Dec: Toller initiates large-scale relief plan to feed civilian population of Spain (known as 'Spanish Relief') secures co-operation of United States and several European countries; raises several million dollars' worth of food supplies. But Franco's victory prevents aid getting through.

1939   Publication of play *Pastor Hall* (premiered in 1947). 28 April: **Hitler denounces German-Polish non-aggression pact and Anglo-German naval treaty.** 22 May: Toller commits suicide in New York.

Introduction

In 1922, while serving a five-year prison sentence for his part in the 1919 November Revolution in Munich, Ernst Toller contributed an autobiographical essay – written in the third person – as a preface to a study of his plays:

Born on 1 December 1893, in Samotschin, near Bromberg [now Bydgoszcz, central Poland]. His father, Max Toller, merchant, died when the boy was 16 . . . After matriculation he is driven to France by that curiosity and longing for the world which had already enticed him on a secret boyhood trip to Bornholm and Denmark. He studies at the university of Grenoble, travels around southern France and northern Italy.

At the end of July 1914 he stops in Lyon en route to Paris. On 31 July the German consul in Lyon, who possesses the same political farsightedness as most representatives of Germany abroad, re-assures his questioner and advises him to travel on to Paris. In the night of 1 August the newsboys' shouts swirl round his ears: 'German declaration of war on Russia – imminent!' He leaves Lyon on the last train to Geneva, is arrested on the journey, released, arrested again, released again, and after an adventurous trip reaches Switzerland a few minutes before the closing of the frontier with France. In Munich he enlists as a volunteer, con-vinced that duty calls him to defend the 'threatened Fatherland'.

As he becomes a soldier, he abandons the traditional circles of the 'middle-class offspring', which he had broken through once before as a thirteen-year-old when he was almost taken to court and expelled from school for writing a newspaper article siding with a workhouse pauper against the authorities.

He sees the 'great times,' but campaigns from the very first day against the orgies of hate and revenge whipped up by the brood of vipers known as hack journalists. Thirteen months' service in the field. He believes in his duty, murders, murders . . . and finds himself in the Priesterwald on a heap of 'French' and 'German' corpses who in gruesome embrace raise their clenched fists against a self-profaning humanity, against a fate which gloats over the dance of death of blind nations.

He is a convalescent, atoning yet laden with guilt, a murderer whose hands can never be cleansed.

As one of the 'war-wounded', he is discharged. For a semester he studies at Munich. Gradually he comes to himself. He is not fatigued, not gnawed away with loathing of the times he lived in, not anxious to avoid contemporary events. He has become a fundamental rebel.

He searches for comrades. He takes part in the 'Culture Congress' at Burg Lauenstein convened by the publisher Diederich, sees the confusion, the cowardice, the despondency of the older generation. Dreamer of reality, he shouts angry words at the betrayers of youth. The decision matures to find revolutionary youth for himself. In the winter of 1917 he studies at Heidelberg and is allowed to be one of Max Weber's students. (One of the few German middle-class professors who was a politician . . . and a character. Which in Germany means even more.) In Heidelberg he finds comrades. He is invited to join a circle of students brought together by a dull, unclarified impulse to discuss contemporary problems, but whose strong and passionate love of truth and justice senses that at this time discussion cannot be the answer.

His call for renunciation of the 'great times' binds the stout hearts together. A cultural-political confederation of German youth is formed, whose programmatic principles have an air of naive and utopian socialism . . . Local groups are formed at other universities. Furiously attacked by the traditional German students' clubs, our confederation fights back – a Don Quixote of 1917. The Supreme Command's infamous intelligence service starts paying attention. Students belonging to the confederation are drafted into military service without any examination . . . Female students of Austrian nationality have to leave Germany. The author succeeds in escaping to Berlin.

Here he gets to know a number of people who think like him. (One or these men is called Kurt Eisner.) He reads the 'underground' political writings of the time and comes to the – to him shattering – conclusion that the German government is not guiltless of the outbreak and continuance of the war, that the German people is being betrayed. He teaches himself about the conduct, aims and strategies of the war, and his way to the proletariat becomes clearer.

In January 1918 he comes to Munich and takes part in the strike of munition workers. 'Reserved' workers, spared from service at the front and employed on high wages, rose up and fought for their European brothers in the field. Peace without any overt or veiled condition and with preservation of the right of self-determination of all peoples, including the Germans – this was the watchword of the proletariat, awakened at last. Following Kurt Eisner's arrest on the first day of the strike, the workers elect the author as a member of the strike committee. He speaks at meetings on the Theresienwiese, takes part in the negotiations with the chief of police which were initiated to obtain Eisner's release – and, after the strike is broken off, is arrested on the charge of 'attempted high treason'. At the same time farcically, and without medical examination, 'kitted out' again.

Months of study in the military prison and under custody in the barracks. Where hitherto he was a revolutionary out of mere sentiment, he now becomes a revolutionary socialist from knowledge.

Transfiguration [*Toller's first play*] *takes its final form on walks in the depressing prison yard.*

The November Revolution draws him to Munich. He is elected chairman of the central council of the workers', peasants' and soldiers' councils, takes part in the sessions of the Bavarian National Council, of the first German Congress of Councils, and of the Bavarian Congress of Councils. The Independent Socialist Party in Munich nominates him chairman of the Party in March 1919. Although himself a believer in the idea of a Räterepublik [*a Republic governed by Councils*], *he at first opposes the proclamation of the Bavarian* Räterepublik, *convinced that the necessary political conditions were lacking at that time. But when the* Räterepublik *had found its outward form in the masses' spontaneous uprising in a number of Bavarian towns, and the proclamation was no longer therefore an act of duty but of control, of mastery of a pre-existing situation, he enters the government of the* Räterepublik *in accord with the Party's resolution. Recognising the fact that Munich was cut off on all sides, recognising the consequences of a bloody suppression of the workers, he tries, towards the end of April, to prepare for the winding up of the* Räterepublik. *In vain. The revolutionary uprising, a last foolhardy attempt by the workers' advance guard to save the lost German November Revolution, is overthrown.*

A premium of 10,000 Marks is placed on the author's head. On 6 June 1919 he is arrested. From 14 to 16 July he is put on trial before a summary court in Munich. They sentence him to five years imprisonment.

Transfiguration, Toller's first play, premiered in Berlin in 1919, is an archetypal Expressionist piece, with anonymous 'types' rather than characters and a string of more or less phantasmagoric scenes or 'stations' (so called in the text). The male protagonist enlists for the Front (I), endures the horrors of trench warfare (II) in a scene that foreshadows the second act of O'Casey's *Silver Tassie*, is hospitalised (III), attempts to return to civilian life (IV), identifies with the exploited workers (V) and leads them to revolutionary action (VI). As Toller himself wrote later:

Every author wants cram into his first work everything he knows, everything he has ever experienced. I did that too . . .

Toller's second play, *Masses and Man*, premiered in Nuremberg in 1920, is also in the Expressionist mode. This time the protagonist is a middle-class woman, Sonja, who renounces her husband and her social position to join the working masses in their struggle. Alternating dream scenes with scenes of abstracted reality, the play contrasts Sonja's advocacy of passive resistance with a call by the Nameless One to violent revolution. The Nameless One prevails. Civil war ensues, the rebellion is bloodily crushed, and Sonja is arrested as instigator. In prison she rejects offers of freedom both from her husband and from the Nameless One, because both involve compromise. But as she goes to her execution past two other prisoners dividing her clothes between them, they hesitate and seem to see the light . . .

The first production was stopped by the police after four performances and banned by the Bavarian Government from further staging because of complaints from the Association of German-Jewish Citizens, who, according to Toller, 'felt themselves insulted by the Stock Exchange scene', in which top-hatted bankers dance a fox-trot as war loans and munitions shares rocket in value.

But the following year *Masses and Man* was successfully staged at the Berlin Volksbühne, then two years later in Moscow by Meyerhold, in April 1924 in New York in a production directed and designed by Lee Simonson and the following month in London by the Stage Society directed by Lewis Casson with Sybil Thorndike in the lead.

The Machine Wreckers, Toller's third play, premiered in Berlin in 1922 in a production designed by John Heartfield, takes up a theme established in *Masses and Man*. Sonja says:

> 'Factories may no longer be the masters
> And men the means.
> Let factories be servants
> Of decent living;
> And let the soul of man
> Conquer the factories.'

In *The Machine Wreckers*, Toller takes the problem of the mechanisation of labour back to its first flashpoint: the Luddite riots in Nottingham in 1815. In his autobiography, published in 1933, Toller returned to the conflicts dramatised in the play:

How easily the masses let themselves, even now, be led and misled by promises, emotions, hopes of self-advantage . . . How easy it becomes for powerful platform orators to rouse them to actions of blind passion. I have come to see the basic social factor which conditions this instability, the great and crippling defect of our time: man's dependence on the labour market and on the machine.

I used to think the power of reason was so strong that anyone recognising it must follow it. But knowledge is forgotten, experience is forgotten . . . and the people are their own worst enemy.

In my play The Machine Wreckers *I try to give shape to these conflicts and the clash between rebels and revolutionaries, and man's perilous struggle with the machine. The history of the Luddites provided me with multifarious parallels.*

On the day of the first performance in Max Reinhardt's Grosses Schauspielhaus in Berlin, Rathenau was murdered by nationalist students. In the last act of the play, when the people, goaded on by a traitor, beat their leader to death, the 5000-strong audience rose up spontaneously and the stage became the tribune of our era.

Rathenau, an advocate of international co-operation, was in fact assassinated six days before the premiere, but the event was still fresh in the audience's minds and the parallel must have been uncanny.

About his sources for the play, Toller wrote in a letter from prison:

I found substantial material for my play, The Machine Wreckers, *in Marx's* Capital *and Engels'* Condition of the Working Classes in England.

An author cannot determine the point at which the material takes shape and becomes his own living property, the point at which experience becomes form. If I am nonetheless having some books sent from London, it is for the purpose of verification and . . . in the hope of finding corroboration in the historical facts. It was several years ago now that I became interested in the Luddite problem.

I can't wait to get Butler's Erewhon. *In my play too, the machine has more than a materialistic significance. It's 'Devil,' 'Demon,' and it's not only the social misery that it causes (unemployment, depression of wages, division of labour) that leads to its destruction, but also its 'nightmarish appearance'. And finally I tried to make the machine a symbol of our mechanistic age.*

That was written before the play reached the stage. After the first production, which he never saw (as was the case with each of his first four plays), he wrote, presumably in response to some adverse criticism of the play on stage:

I am not responsible for any vandalism, red-pencillings and saccharine melodramatics in the production, and, as long as I am sitting here in prison, I have no influence on the way the play is presented. Any comparison with The Weavers [*by Gerhart*

Hauptmann, 1892] is lame. When I wrote The Machine Wreckers, *I had not read* The Weavers *for twelve years; in fact, I had never read it, but, as a boy, I had seen it performed in a provincial theatre. I deliberately shunned reading it at that time. All I remembered was the tragedy of the unenlightened masses made rebellious by hunger and despair. I wanted (among other things) to give expression to the first awakening of the people to revolutionary consciousness.*

In periods of the sharpest social conflicts, the theatre will reflect those conflicts. The proletarian in today's drama is no longer the proletarian of the nineteenth century. He no longer breathes the hopeless and stagnating, albeit shocking air of The Lower Depths *[by Maxim Gorky, 1902]. The nineteenth-century proletarian suffered blindly under the burden of his fate from want, exploitation, excessive toil and meagre rewards. The twentieth-century proletarian has become a conscious fighter, a defender of an idea. Not content merely to criticise, he creates images of new realities which he will build. His language, influenced by the party newspaper's leading articles, is poor in strong images, rich in dialectical acuity. Put him on stage and it is hardly surprising if he repels those who are his enemies in real life. In* The Machine Wreckers, *I tried to show the evolution of this new type of proletarian.*

The fourth play Toller wrote in prison was *Hinkemann*, premiered in Leipzig in 1923. Owing a debt to Büchner's *Woyzeck*, Toller's protagonist is a 'Heimkehrer', a soldier returning home from the front, and one who in this case has been rendered impotent by the injuries he's sustained. Rejected by his wife, Hinkemann is forced to earn his living as a fairground strongman with a speciality in drinking live rats' blood. Things go from bad to worse, and the play ends with both Hinkemann and his wife committing suicide.

The second German production, in Dresden in January 1924, provoked a riot amongst the nationalists, and questions were asked in parliament. These were inflammatory times. There had been Communist uprisings the previous October, and the following month Hitler had staged his beer-hall putsch in Munich – and was now in jail ...

Hinkemann was seen in Moscow in the autumn of 1923, in London at the Gate Theatre in 1926 and in the USA in 1930.

Having served every day of his five-year sentence, Toller was released from prison on 15 July 1924. Expelled from Bavaria, he found himself much in demand from literary, political and trades union circles in the rest of Germany as well as in Czechoslovakia, the Near East, England, the Soviet Union and Scandinavia. A cease-

less round of lectures, guest appearances, speeches, readings and
attendances at productions of his plays left no time for writing new
ones. So it was not until September 1927 that *Hoppla! Such is Life!*
was premiered (almost) simultaneously in Hamburg and Berlin.
The Berlin production, at the Volksbühne, was by Erwin Piscator.

A succession of episodic scenes, interspersed with 'cinemato-
graphic interludes', *Hoppla!* takes its hero on a tour of contemporary Germany, following his release after eight years in a mental
asylum for 'revolutionary activity'. He finds his erstwhile
comrades have mostly sold out, while corruption and inhumanity
are all-pervasive. He reaches his point of no return when serving as
a waiter in the Grand Hotel, rendered in Piscator's production by a
massive, four-storey constructivist cross-section, providing seven
separate acting areas and as many different projection surfaces. He
is arrested and pronounced insane again. He hangs himself in his
cell only moments before his innocence is proved.

Although Toller wrote some six more plays after *Hoppla!*, they
none of them made the same impact as his earlier work. As he
himself half admits, contact with the real world seems paradox-
ically to have stultified the imagination that could be given free
rein in prison. He continued travelling (to America and Republican
Spain) and working for socialism in the face of the rising tide of
Nazism, until he fled Germany after the Reichstag fire. He lived in
Britain on and off from February 1934 until October 1936 and
attended the British premieres of three of his plays, co-directing a
fourth himself: *Draw the Fires!* at the Manchester Opera House in
February 1935, with music by Hanns Eisler. He also got married in
England – to the actress Christine Grautoff.

Moving to the USA, like many other exiled writers Toller spent
time in Hollywood working on scripts for MGM, but much of his
energy went into organising millions of dollars' worth of civilian
relief for the Spanish Civil War – which ultimately failed to get
through. Germany had already annexed Austria, and in April 1938
Hitler renounced the Anglo-German naval treaty and Germany's
non-aggression pact with Poland. A new war must have seemed
inevitable.

Toller hanged himself in his New York hotel on 22 May 1939.
Christopher Isherwood, who had been to see him only six weeks
before, as he wrote later in *Exhumations*, had been 'struck by the
change in his appearance, and in his manner. He looked older,
yellower, thinner. The black eyes were sombre, and almost gentle.
And his pleasure at my visit was quite touching.'

*Compiled and translated by Nicholas Hern. Excerpts from Toller's
writings copyright the Estate of Ernst Toller.*

THE MACHINE WRECKERS

The Royal National Theatre's revival of *The Machine Wreckers* opened at the Cottesloe Theatre on 11 August 1995, with the following cast:

Prologue

LORD CHANCELLOR OF ENGLAND	Richard Bremmer
LORD BYRON	Colin Tierney
LORD CASTLEREAGH	John McEnery

JIMMY COBBETT	Colin Tierney
FIRST BOY	John Rogan
FIRST GIRL	Lizzie McPhee
TEDDY WIBLEY	Nick Bagnall
SECOND GIRL	Elaine Claxton
SECOND BOY	Crispin Letts
JOHN WIBLEY	Ron Cook
WEAVERS	Jude Akuwudike, Richard Bremmer, Bríd Brennan, Henry Ian Cusick, Paola Dionisotti, John McEnery, Danny Sapani, Jonathan Slinger, Jem Wall
NED LUD	Declan Conlon
PEDLAR	Crispin Letts
BEGGAR	Karl Johnson
FIRST DRUNKARD	Danny Sapani
SECOND DRUNKARD	Jonathan Slinger
CHARLES	Jem Wall
THE TOWN CRIER	Richard Bremmer
MRS COBBETT, *mother of Henry and Jimmy*	Paola Dionisotti
HENRY COBBETT	Crispin Letts
OLD REAPER	John Rogan
TEDDY WIBLEY	Nick Bagnall
MARY, *Old Reaper's daughter*	Elaine Claxton
BOB	Lizzie McPhee
WILLIAM	Jude Akuwudike
EDWARD	Danny Sapani
GEORGE	Jonathan Slinger
ARTHUR	Henry Ian Cusick

ALBERT	Richard Bremmer
URE, *a manufacturer*	John McEnery
URE'S DAUGHTER	Lizzie McPhee
URE'S GUEST	John Rogan
MAN WITH A BARROW	Jem Wall
DEAF AND DUMB PERSON	Paola Dionisotti
BLIND PERSON	Henry Ian Cusick
FIRST GIRL	Danny Sapani
SECOND GIRL	Elaine Claxton
FIRST BOY	Nick Bagnall
SECOND BOY	Jonathan Slinger
THIRD BOY	Jude Akuwudike
FIRST WOMAN	Paola Dionisotti
SECOND WOMAN	Lizzie McPhee
THIRD WOMAN	Jem Wall
FOURTH WOMAN	Richard Bremmer
FIFTH WOMAN	Henry Ian Cusick
MARGARET LUD	Bríd Brennan
YOUNG LUD	Jonathan Slinger
PROSTITUTE	Nick Bagnall
ENGINEER	Crispin Letts
FOREMAN	Colin Tierney

Directed by Katie Mitchell
Designed by Vicki Mortimer
Lighting by Tina MacHugh
Music by Helen Chadwick
Movement Director Paul Allain
Company Voice Work Patsy Rodenburg
Sound by Sue Patrick

Persons of the Prologue
LORD CHANCELLOR OF ENGLAND.
LORD BYRON.
LORD CASTLEREAGH.
Other Peers.

Persons of the Play
JIMMY COBBETT.
JOHN WIBLEY,
CHARLES,
BOB,
WILLIAM,
EDWARD,   } *weavers.*
ARTHUR,
GEORGE,
NED LUD,
A Pedlar.
A Beggar.
Two Drunkards.
An Officer.
HENRY COBBETT, *overseer.*
MRS COBBETT, *mother of Henry and Jimmy.*
OLD REAPER.
TEDDY WIBLEY.
MARY WIBLEY, *Old Reaper s daughter.*
URE, *a manufacturer.*
Ure's little daughter.
Man with a Barrow.
Deaf and Dumb Man.
Blind Man.
Women Weavers.
Children.
MARGARET LUD.
YOUNG LUD.
A Streetwalker.
Ure's Guest.
An Engineer.

The scene is laid in London and Nottingham, about the years 1812-15.

Prologue

The House of Lords, 1812. In the middle the LORD
CHANCELLOR *on the woolsack. To right and left of him
seats for* LORD BYRON *and* LORD CASTLEREAGH; *in
the first row of the theatre sit other peers.*

LORD CHANCELLOR. A Government Bill to render the
    destruction of machinery punishable by death. The Bill was
    passed by a majority at the first reading. We will proceed to
    the second and third readings. – Lord Byron.

LORD BYRON. All of you know, my lords, why we are met.
    The working weavers are confederate
    Against their masters; they have used duress
    And plan destruction. But whose policy
    Taught them the trade of havoc, whose the hand
    That undermined the welfare of the realm?
    It was the policy of robber wars,
    The myth of heroes from your history books,
    That grew to be the curse of living men!
    O, can you wonder, lords, if in these times
    When fraud and shameless greed like mildew tarnish
    Our highest ranks, the working folk forget
    The duty that they owe the State, and add
    Guilt to the burden of their penury?
    Theirs is a crime, my lords, I grant, and yet
    Such deeds are daily done in Parliament
    The evildoer in high places knows
    How to slip through the meshes of the law:
    The workman does his penance for the crime
    That hunger, hunger drove him to commit.
    Machinery stole ground beneath his feet,

Thrust him relentless on the road to want.
Rebellion cried within him:
Nature demands that all shall live!
Nature denies that some must feast
While others famish! Noble lords,
The labourer stood in readiness
To till the fallow fields of England;
Only the spade he held was not his own.
 He was a beggar. Who rose up
And said: We help you in your need?
Blind passion was the end for all of us.
You call these men and women rabble,
Cry out upon the many-headed monster,
Demand its leaders shall be straightway hanged.
Where Mercy starves, the State must thirst for blood.
The sword, as ever, is a shift of fools
To hide their folly.
Let us consider well this rabble, lords:
It is the rabble digging in your fields,
It is the rabble serving in your halls,
It is the rabble whence your soldiers spawn,
It is the strong arm that sets you in power
To bid defiance to an enemy world,
And it will bid defiance to its masters
If it be driven madly to despair.
And one thing more I say to you, my lords,
For wars your purse was ever open wide;
A tenth part of the money that you gave
To Portugal in 'service of mankind'
Would have sufficed to still the pangs at home
And give the gallows peace. I saw in Turkey
The most despotic rule the world has known,
But nowhere dearth in plenty such as here
In Christian England.
And what is now your remedy for the ill?
Hanging, the nostrum of all penny-quacks
Who burrow in the body of the State!
Is not the law bespattered to the crown?
Shall blood be shed until it steams to Heaven
In witness of your guilt? Is hanging medicine

For hunger and despair? Suppose, my lords,
Your bill made law. Regard the prisoner
Brought up for judgment, dull with misery,
Weak with starvation, weary of a life
That by your reckoning is of less account
Than one dismantled loom. Regard this man,
Torn from the family whose breadwinner
He may not be (although the will is there),
Dragged into court. Who will pronounce the verdict?
Twelve honest men and true? Never, my lords!
Command twelve butchers as your jurymen,
And make a hangman judge!

Ironical laughter has broken out among the peers.

LORD CHANCELLOR. Lord Castlereagh.

LORD CASTLEREAGH. You have heard, my lords,
    The speech of this most honourable peer.
    His was a poet's voice, and not a statesman's.
    Poets may dream in verses and write dramas,
    But statecraft is the business of hard men.
    It is a poet's licence to espouse
    The cause of vagabondage; statesmen stand
    By principle alone. Poverty is a law
    Of God and Nature, and compassionate scruples
    Must have no place in legislators' minds.
    The reverend Malthus showed that scores of thousands
    Too many live in England, and the earth denies
    Bread to the masses that encumber her.
    The miseries we see are God-ordained
    And we must bow in silence to His Will.
    Plague, war, and famine yearly rid the world
    Of needless burdens. Shall we combat Nature?
    That would be criminal. We must accept
    The world we know, the law we comprehend,
    And aid them with the power we can dispose.
    The more we help the poor, the more they breed.
    They *must* not multiply on England's soil!
    And every means that hinders them is just,
    If only it accord with moral practice
    And Divine precept.

LORD BYRON.   Let the children starve!

LORD CASTLEREAGH. Your *beau geste*, my lord, we must
     admire,
  But as a statesman I reply with coldness,
  The more the infant ranks are thinned by Death
  The better for our children and our land.
  There are too many of us, honoured poet;
  An iron fact that all our sympathy
  Can never soften. I would beg my lords
  Consider one thing only, that the welfare
  Of England is at stake. Plots are afoot
  To break the quiet of our peaceful realm.
   If Justice have a temple, let me lay
  This bill upon her altar, confident
  That sober statecraft will outweigh the voice
  Of poetry and passion.

Applause of the peers.

LORD CHANCELLOR. The debate is ended. We will proceed
  to a division. Those noble lords in favour of the Bill? (*All
  but* LORD BYRON *rise.*) Those against? (LORD BYRON
  rises in his place. Laughter.) I observe one vote. The bill is
  passed. The sitting is adjourned until to-morrow.

The stage darkens. End of the prologue.

The First Act

A street in Nottingham on a sunny day in Spring. Children with pinched and wan faces, in ragged clothes, squat dully round a wooden framework in the shape of gallows.

JIMMY COBBETT, *in mechanic's clothes, comes from a side street and looks on.*

JIMMY. What, idle all? Is this a holiday?

FIRST BOY. The guys are to be hanged.

JIMMY. The guys?

FIRST GIRL. Yes, guys. They're hidden in the house of Weaver John.

SECOND BOY. I've seen them.

JIMMY. Are all of you at drudgery so young?

FIRST BOY. My brother, four years old, stands at the loom.

FIRST GIRL. Teddy can hardly walk and earns three pence a day; three real pennies.

> SECOND GIRL *begins to cry.*

JIMMY. Why are you crying, little one? (*She does not answer.*) Tell me, for I keep secrets.

SECOND GIRL. O, sir, I can t tell . . . but the sun's so warm to-day!

JIMMY (*after a silence*). Children, do you know any games?

FIRST GIRL. We are so hungry, sir!

JIMMY. Do you love fairy tales?

SECOND BOY. 'Fairy tales,' what are those?

JIMMY. Strange tales of far-off lands of wonder,
Tales of bright meadows where the children play.

SECOND GIRL. Oh, play! Tell us one, sir!

JIMMY. A rich man – Golden Belly was his name –
   With several castles all as big and fine
   As Mr Ure's new house up on the hill,
    Lived with an only daughter he called Joy.
   She wore a golden frock, and played all day
   With golden playthings in a golden garden.

FIRST BOY. With golden playthings?

FIRST GIRL. Was she never at the loom?

JIMMY. Never. The man was rich, his child called Joy.
   And not far from their castle lived a weaver
   Who also had an only child, called Sorrow,
   A meagre boy with puny chest and legs
   Like sally-rods – a starveling such as thou.
   And one day little Sorrow, with a load
   Of linen in a basket on his arm
   Came to the castle door. He saw the golden toys,
   The golden garden –

The THIRD BOY *has crept aside to rummage in the gutter.*

THIRD BOY. Hurrah, I've found a crust!

FIRST GIRL. Give us a bite!

FIRST BOY. You cheat! We listen and you look for bread!
   That isn't fair! Give here! We'll share it!

The children wrestle with the THIRD BOY.

THIRD BOY. I won't! I won't! I'll bite you – see!

SECOND BOY. Bite, will you! I'll teach you to bite!

There is a scuffle for the crust. The THIRD BOY *runs away, and the others chase him.*

JIMMY. Called Joy . . . called Sorrow . . .

From a side street comes a procession of weavers, men and women, in ragged clothes. Some of the men wear paper caps. In front are held aloft three guys or puppets representing strike-breakers. Uproar. JOHN WIBLEY *mounts a step at the base of the gallows.*

JOHN WIBLEY (*to the guys*). Turncoats and traitors! Scabs of
  master's men!
   Blacklegs and varlets! Greedy wolfish pack
   That lap the hunger-sweat of poverty!
   With one accord we took our stand to strike,
   No hand's turn at machines! And then these toads,
   These buttock-men went creeping to the mill
   To beg the favour of a place! May Hell
   Devour your flesh, and twist your bones with tongs,
   May Nightmare grind a hoof upon your hearts,
   Your gullets be enlac'd with knotted cords
   Dipped in hot oil! May you be put in chains
   Before a liquor-vat, and when your tongues are dry
   See wrinkled hags befoul your drinking-pot!

*The guys are hanged amid plaudits. Two weavers take place
to right and left of the gallows, and sing in a monotone.*

FIRST WEAVER. They served the master, but betrayed the man.

SECOND WEAVER. So hang them high!

FIRST WEAVER. They broke their faith and kneeled at
  Mammon's throne.

SECOND WEAVER. So hang them high!

FIRST WEAVER. They sold their bodies and befouled their
  minds.

SECOND WEAVER. So hang them high!

FIRST WEAVER. If they're in Heaven, who can be in Hell?

SECOND WEAVER. They shall not come to Heaven. Hang
  them high!

CHORUS (*dancing round the gallows*). Ba, ba, black sheep!
  Ba, ba, black sheep!

FIRST WEAVER. Blackleg, Blackleg, have you any wool?

SECOND WEAVER. Yes, sir, yes, sir, three bags full.
  One for the master, one for the man,
  And one for the trimmers who serve whom they can.

  Chorus – Ba, ba, black sheep!
  Ba, ba, black sheep!

FIRST WEAVER. Down, down, down and down,
　　Pauper and drudge and slave!
　　From moor and meadow, street and loom,
　　From sty and dunghill, hutch and tomb,
　　Hark to the thunder-call of doom:
　　Work or the grave!

SECOND WEAVER. Out, out, out and out
　　With despot, tyrant, waster!
　　What, shall we toil for idlers' gain?
　　Who will not work with might and main
　　Is England's curse and freedom's bane;
　　Our right is master!

The weavers pull up the beams of the gallows, and go off singing.

SONG.
　　On, on, on and on,
　　The coward's day is past!
　　The night is flown, the dawn is bright,
　　The measure's full, the sands are light,
　　The battle joined, the end in sight;
　　Who will stand fast?

　　NED LUD *and* CHARLES *remain.*

NED LUD. I'll wager that not ten of them have shirts to their
　　backs.

A pedlar comes, crying his wares.

PEDLAR. Parr's Life Pills! Parr's Life Pills! No weaver need
　　starve. Without bite or sup they make you look like
　　England's queen. Parr's Life Pills! Parr's Life Pills!

An old beggar comes, looking for crusts.

BEGGAR. I can see well this is no working day. The children –
　　devil's brood – have swallowed all. (*He comes to* JIMMY.)
　　Sir, give me a halfpenny.

JIMMY. I am a man as poor as you. An out-of-work, a tramp,
　　wellnigh starving.

BEGGAR. The man for my money then. Do you think I would

beg from a bladder of lard? If there were none but rich on
this earth, all beggars would famish. The poor share and
share alike. That's how they come to Heaven.

JIMMY. How so?

BEGGAR. Know you not the words of the Lord Jesus? It is
easier for a camel to pass through the eye of a needle, than
for a rich man to enter the Kingdom. The rich are close and
love not giving; that is why they grow pot-bellied. The gate
of the Kingdom is narrow; just big enough for shrunken
starvelings like our poor. And the gate is low. A tall man
such as you can scarce pass through for the cap he wears.
You stand in peril of damnation.

JIMMY (*giving him his cap*). Friend, you have missed your
calling. You should have been a parson, or a Parliament
man.

BEGGAR. 'Tis true, I am no common beggar. I am a beggar
with a greed for renown. I am looking for the man who will
give me land worth three hundred pounds sterling. Once,
long ago, I saw Westminster Palace from the street; and the
fancy takes me to see it from within. Farewell, friend. The
sun loves men as young as you, and it is no more than
courtesy to bare the head to a lover.

JIMMY. Your love is the bottle, it seems. And I fear my cap
will go over the potman's counter.

BEGGAR. Friend, you are an Irishman. You have eaten too
many potatoes. They work windily on the stomach, and the
bad air is belched in moralizing. Get you a pig instead. But
don't mate with him. They say the Irish love their pigs so
dearly that they sleep with them. That way lies the breeding
of pigheads; and we have enough of them in England
already.

The BEGGAR *goes off. Two drunkards come in, arm in
arm.*

FIRST DRUNKARD (*sings*).
Sharpen the scythe! The corn is ripe,
The children cry for bread.
The fields are watered with their tears,

Dunged by their fathers' dead!
When hands were cold and hearts were numb
The winter seed was spread.

SECOND DRUNKARD. Blessed are the poor in spirit, saith
the Lord. And to whom He loveth, He giveth. What, are we
poor in spirit? Gin, gin for my penny! Hast a penny, brother?

FIRST DRUNKARD. A penny! Ha, ha! Where kings line their
closets with the gold of the Easterlings! I have a hundred
shillings, man – in my belly! My wife drinks gin with me –
and my children too . . . They can take their bottle – ha, ha!
– better than you! The youngest takes gin from the breast –
gin – gin –

BOTH DRUNKARDS (*singing*). Gin – gin – gin – gin –

They pass on. JIMMY *comes up* to NED LUD.

JIMMY. YOU are Ned Lud?

NED LUD. So they call me. And you?

JIMMY. A workman like yourself.

NED LUD. From Nottingham?

JIMMY. Nottingham born and bred. For years a vagabond;
now back again for the first time. I wandered over England
and the Continent.

NED LUD. I greet you then as comrade on your home-coming.

JIMMY. Thank you, Ned Lud . . . The weavers are on strike?

CHARLES. The steam-engine is in the town!

NED LUD. They seek to press us into fearful slavery!

JIMMY. Therefore the fight?

NED LUD. They would put us in irons, and chain us to a
monster. A spindle driven by steam that clutches men and
whirls them round and slings them into hell!

JIMMY. The spinning-mule is in the village.

NED LUD. Every man on God's earth has a right to live by the
work of his hands. Every man is born free, and has a right to
a trade . . . A holy right! Whoever robs him of it is a thief!

The masters betrayed us when they brought the
steam-engine into the town! What does our handicraft count
for now?

JIMMY. But you had the spinning-jenny?

CHARLES. That was the first offence against our rights.

NED LUD. One weaver worked three spindles; the jenny
drives eighteen. It robs five weavers of their daily bread. A
thousand spindles, so they say, are driven by the mule. Now
comes the day when Ure would lead us to the knackers'
yard. 'Hey, slaughter all the pack! I have the steam-engine!'
We must stand together. No hand's turn at machines! We
would live by the work of our hands, as we have always
done. We are men! Engine-wages are devil's wages. We
have joined hands. John Wibley is our leader. To-night we
meet in session at his house.

JIMMY. And you make war on the machines?

NED LUD. Our fists are still our own!

JIMMY. I know the steam-engine, and say that what you plan
is madness!

NED LUD. Mad though it be, vain though it be, we must fight,
for we are men! If we endure the yoke we are no more than
brutes.

JIMMY. I know that this machine is our inevitable lot – our
destiny.

NED LUD. Your words are strange to me.

JIMMY. I will open your blind eyes. I go with you to Weaver
Wibley. There let me speak.

NED LUD. See, here come soldiers!

*From a side street comes a platoon of soldiers, followed by
a crowd.*

THE OFFICER. By the King's Majesty it is proclaim'd –
Now doff your caps, you ill-condition'd pack! –
That high authority is made aware
Of leagues in secret join'd by lawless men
Against the peace and order of this realm.

Therefore *We do prohibit* all endeavour
By faction to increase the proper wage
Or lessen the appointed hours of labour.
We do prohibit every let or hindrance
To diligent subjects in their lawful trade,
Whether by threat, persuasion, or request.
We do forbid all workmen to forsake
In common cause their service or employ.
We do forbid the hoarding up of gold
For times when strikers shall abandon duty.
We do allow the honourable masters
By their own measure to decree the wage
And working hour. For those who disobey
Our mandate, *We ordain* a penalty
Up to, but not above, ten years' imprisonment.
Those faithful subjects who inform the law
Of secret leagues, and show the hiding-place
Of wrongful and forbidden funds, receive
The half of all such monies in reward.
The other half is forfeit to the Crown.
Let all men go their ways. God Save the King!

Flourish of trumpets. The soldiers march off.

NED LUD. Half for brother Judas, half for brother King. An
honourable share indeed!

Curtain.

The Second Act

Scene One

A parlour, where HENRY COBBETT *and his mother are at their midday meal.*

HENRY. I hate this onion-sauce, this gutter-seasoning!

MOTHER (*meekly*). Your father always –

HENRY. Father! Father! I know his style. The dainty dish at the wedding breakfast – roast beef with onion sauce! Then onions for Christmas, Easter, Whitsun. Father had no enemy but himself.

MOTHER. His wages –

HENRY. Nonsense. Want of ability. He remained a stocking-weaver to the end. I was an overseer by thirty. Mark the difference! Let us drop the subject. The thought of those days turns the stomach sour.

    JIMMY *enters.*

JIMMY. Mother!

MOTHER. My boy! To see you once again –

JIMMY. Good day, Henry.

HENRY. So you have grown into a man – at last. To judge by your clothes you've little else to boast of.

MOTHER. You must be tired and hungry. Sit with us.

    JIMMY *seats himself.*

JIMMY. You're fine and cosy here.

HENRY. What is your profession?

JIMMY. A tramp, mechanic, out-of-work.

HENRY. That's no profession.

JIMMY. I'm a workman. A weaver.

HENRY. That's no honour.

JIMMY. The Queen has not a greater in her gift.

HENRY. A strange sort of honour – to be a gutter-snipe!

JIMMY. Do you call yourself a gutter-snipe? The bird fouls its own nest.

HENRY. You're making a mistake.

MOTHER. Henry's not a weaver now. He's worked his way right up. He's overseer for Mr Ure.

JIMMY. If he abuses workmen, he abuses me.

HENRY. It's not my fault my brother is a vagabond.

JIMMY. And why do you live at ease and eat your bellyful? Because the vagabonds give their strength, their lives.

HENRY. A law of Nature. If the strong are to live, the weak must go to the wall. Do you ask me to *sink* again? Do you ask me to let go what I have won?

MOTHER. You'll stay in Nottingham, Jimmy?

JIMMY. I came in time, it seems. The weavers are on strike.

HENRY (*sharply*). What's that?

JIMMY. They claim their rights as men.

HENRY. Words! Phrases!

JIMMY. Is misery a phrase? Starvation? Or child drudgery?

HENRY. You are a rebel.

JIMMY. If love of justice is rebellion, yes.

HENRY. You must leave Nottingham

JIMMY. There's no call to go.

HENRY. But my position –

JIMMY. No concern of mine.

HENRY. A pretty guest we're entertaining, mother!

MOTHER. Jimmy, you're not in earnest?

JIMMY. Never more in earnest, mother.

HENRY. Look at the rabble you would make your friends. On Sunday, the Lord's Day, they roll from one pothouse to the next. The womenfolk are on the streets, girls of twelve sell themselves at every corner. The children steal. Not long ago the police dragged the Trent for a child's body and found sixty! Sixty murdered children!

JIMMY. Who were the fathers? You and your like, your gentlemen with cash to buy your fancy. Why did the mothers throw their holy babes into the river? Because not one of the fathers stood by them! Because your church makes a shame of their miracle and an infamy of their honour. Why do the men lie drunk in the inns? Because their houses are stinking hutches, fit for brutes! The workmen are better than their masters. For every child who goes hungry, for every man in rags, for every roofless, homeless vaga-bond, for every living soul that cries for beauty and freedom and is driven to live in squalor, you must answer at the reckoning!

HENRY. The weavers are in league against the engine. Do you justify that crime?

JIMMY. Workmen will make themselves the masters of machinery!

HENRY. Then I've said all. Go your way, I'll go mine. I shall disown you well enough. No kith nor kin of mine. No kith nor kin. Mother, now take your choice.

HENRY *leaves the room.*

MOTHER (*after a silence, with an effort*). No – my boy – no! To go back to the old life, the old misery – no! I can't! The hungry years, the bitter winters – no! To count the pence to buy potatoes – no! And the dirt! The rags! I'm old and ill. Don't ask me, for I can't!

JIMMY. That means you're sending me away?

MOTHER (*sobbing*). I'm over sixty. To live it all again – no, no!

She goes out. JIMMY *alone, then the* BEGGAR.

BEGGAR. Charity, kind sir!

JIMMY. The sight of you is a charity, friend, though you come out of time.

BEGGAR. No time is ever out of time, says worldly wisdom. When Time rides an Arab, he runs overtime, and when he straddles an old nag, he's killing time. But when he mounts a wench, then 'tis breeding-time. Has your sweetheart sent you packing?

JIMMY. Mother and brother sent me packing. Mother and brother.

BEGGAR. Old Age and Middle Age, friend. You might have fared worse. It was Youth who showed *me* the door. My son found no call to harbour cripples; he was for every man earning his keep. He found it was my merry sport that set him in this world; and now 'twas his turn to dance. He found me irksome. There, maybe, he was right.

JIMMY. Then you and I can shake hands.

BEGGAR. Aye, so we can. Is that your dinner on the table? I'll take it as an earnest of good-will – though you forgot your manners and didn't ask me. And what will you be – a beggar?

JIMMY. No, friend, I must work. We have a fight before us. The weavers are up and on the march.

BEGGAR. So you would lead them, would you? Then it will be my turn to be breadwinner for us both. Workmen as good Samaritans – I want no better. But workmen as masters – there you'll see miracles indeed! The mill-owners set the Spanish fly on your breast; but the weavers will set three – one on your breast, one on your hips, and one no matter where. I wish you joy of their service!

JIMMY. You're bitter.

BEGGAR. Say truthful, friend.

JIMMY. All men may not be like your son.

BEGGAR. Friend, friend of mine, have you a roof to-night?

JIMMY. No.

BEGGAR. Then let me offer you the state-room in my palace.
You shall be guest of honour there. Lord Rat shall be your
valet, and Lady Louse prepare your bath, and Mistress
Flea-in-Waiting be your merry bed-fellow.

JIMMY. Show me your lodging. I have grave affairs to settle
this evening. Then I will come to you.

The stage is darkened.

Scene Two

A room in JOHN WIBLEY'S *cottage, furnished with a table,
two broken-down chairs, and two weaving stools.* OLD
REAPER *at the window and* TEDDY.)

OLD REAPER. For it is written: As I live, saith the Lord. To
me every knee shall bow, and every tongue confess that I am
Lord. And here stands one whose knees are not bowed, and
whose tongue does not confess him.

TEDDY. Grandpa, I am so hungry!

OLD REAPER. Does He let you hunger?

TEDDY. Grandpa! (*A silence.*) Grandpa, I want to be able to run
like Mr Ure's little girl. But my legs – look at them! (*A silence.*)
If I had bread to eat, oh, then I'd play! (*A silence.*) Grandpa,
why don't you give me bread? I'm hungry, hungry . . .

OLD REAPER. But I have none, I have none! He – up there –
has it all, all! He up there! He lets the just famish and the
unjust live in feasting. O Thou, Thou Murderer of children!
But wait, Teddy, wait! The day of deeds will come! A fight
for life and death – for life and death. Teddy, where's my
gun?

TEDDY. Here, Grandpa, here's the stick.

OLD REAPER. That's no stick, Teddy, that's a gun. I know
One who must fall. (*He takes the stick and aims upward. He
makes as if to pull a trigger, and lets the stick drop.*

Whimpering.) The trigger's rusted. It – won't – fire!

TEDDY. Grandpa, have you seen the steam engine? They say it has a hundred heads.

OLD REAPER. Perhaps it is God. It may be God. Where – where is the engine?

TEDDY. I'll take you to see it, if you like. But not a word to father. Do you promise?

OLD REAPER. Take Me. Take me to it. I may be on His track.

TEDDY. To-morrow night – when father's fast asleep.

Enter JOHN WIBLEY.

JOHN WIBLEY. Mother not in yet?

TEDDY. No, father.

JOHN WIBLEY. The gun again, old fellow? You'll not hit the mark.

OLD REAPER. The wise in their own conceit have become fools.

JOHN WIBLEY *laughs.*

TEDDY. Father, there's a molehill in the yard. Shall we catch the mole?

JOHN WIBLEY. Let the creature live.

OLD REAPER. There, it's in order. My gun, my precious . . .

MARY, a *young handsome woman, comes in.*

MARY. Evening, all.

JOHN WIBLEY. Did Cobbett pay your wages?

MARY (*throwing money on the table*). Fivepence.

JOHN WIBLEY. The cur! The cur!

MARY. Leave me the half. We've not a loaf to eat. Last week I gave you all I earned – and all I made as well.

JOHN WIBLEY. See – not a penny left.

MARY. Have you been gaming?

JOHN WIBLEY. And if I had? I would go whoring if I were a gentleman. I don't need money for myself.

MARY. The thatch is leaky. Rain drips on us in the night. Wet straw. I have no money; 'tis your weavers take it all. Not one of them comes near us but to draw his pay.

JOHN WIBLEY. Debts at the grocer's?

MARY. Five shillings. Oh, this poor man's cheat! Mixing the sugar with the grounds of rice, the flour with chalk and plaster! When Margaret's babe was sick and she bought cocoa, at a thieving price, she found red earth and mutton-fat rubbed into it!

JOHN WIBLEY. Have you got supper?

MARY. A couple of potatoes, if you want them.

JOHN WIBLEY. Later. Now, Mary, come, be sensible. Go to him, play the lover, let him kiss you. Without your help I lose my standing with the men. He gives you money. Do as he bids, and see the wages paid before you kiss. Paid in advance, remember! The comrades come to-night. You're in the way at home.

MARY. Oh God! I'll do it, yes, I'll do it. This life of ours! Come, Teddy, off to bed and sleep. When you wake up you'll find a fresh loaf on your pillow. Good night, father. Sleep well.

OLD REAPER. Bathe thy limbs in balsam, daughter. For the day draws near when thou shalt be crowned queen among daughters.

MARY. With thorns, father.

She goes out.

JOHN WIBLEY. Courage, old man, the day of deeds will come!

Enter CHARLES, BOB, WILLIAM, EDWARD, ARTHUR, GEORGE, *and other workmen.*

CHARLES. It stands in place in the great weaving-shed!

BOB. A Juggernaut. All arms and gaping jaws!

WILLIAM. A monster made to tear us limb from limb!

EDWARD. This is the devil that the masters serve!

GEORGE. With us for wages!

ALL. Aye, with us for wages!

OLD REAPER. They have forsaken the straight road and gone astray.

JOHN WIBLEY. Silence, old fool. Let us take counsel, neighbours. The masters snap their fingers at our strike.

OLD REAPER *goes* out.

CHARLES. In church their parsons thunder, and they set the women at our throats!

BOB. The King makes outlaws of all secret leagues.

JOHN WIBLEY. May the last King be strangled with the bowels
Of the last parson!

CHARLES. Amen to that, say I.

BOB. But what comes next?

JOHN WIBLEY. Are all our sentries posted?

CHARLES. A hundred yards around they stand and watch.

JOHN WIBLEY. Ure held us for his chattels, to be bought,
Worn threadbare, thrown away. Now the machine
Stands in our place, and mastery turns to madness
This hellish engine-monster every day
Devours the wages of a thousand men.

CHARLES. The man who steals our work sins against Nature!

CRIES. Sins against Nature!

JOHN WIBLEY. They plan to hunt the men from every town
And chain the children to their devilments. 'Tis said this engine runs for babes of three.

ALBERT. And if they leave us at the engine, what sort of drudgery will it be? We shall tie up broken threads and tend the hungry beast like prentice farmhands!

EDWARD. No longer weavers. Men without a trade.

JOHN WIBLEY. Ure has sold you to the devil! Can you call
    yourselves your own?

ARTHUR. What will become of us?

ALBERT. Three days I let them chain me to the engine
    In Carlton, then I fled. This devil Steam
    Clutches you in a vice and tears
    The heart from out the breast.
    And then he saws and saws and saws
    The living body into pieces.
    Charles, you shall be the Foot, to tread,
    To tread, to tread your life away . . .
    With slacken'd arms and clouded eyes
    And back bent crooked at the mill.
    George, you shall be the Hand, to tie
    And knot and fasten, knot and tie,
    With deafen'd ears and creeping blood
    And dry-rot in the brain . . .

CHARLES. With slacken'd arms, with clouded eyes –

GEORGE. With deafen'd ears, with creeping blood –

WILLIAM. What if the engine stops, and Master Steam
    Quits work? Then where are Hand and Foot and drudge?

JOHN WIBLEY. Ravens, tame ravens that the master drives
    Into a winter's night, to freeze and die! To freeze and die!

CHARLES. But we are men!

JOHN WIBLEY. We were, once on a time.

CHARLES. It must not be! Why, 'tis a mortal sin!

GEORGE. A curse on Steam!

EDWARD. Ten plagues!

WILLIAM. Bound hand and foot!

OTHERS (*dully*). Bound hand and foot!

JOHN WIBLEY. One way is left. We must defy the engine.
    A Moloch stands in Nottingham. Strike him down!
    A monster that will breed his hateful kind

In thousands! Swear defiance here and now!

WEAVERS. We swear it!

JOHN WIBLEY. Let Moloch welter once in his black blood,
And Ure will never dare to make us fast
To such another Hell-spawn!
Death to the engine, comrades!
War on the tyrant Steam!
Death to the engine!
War on the tyrant Steam!

WEAVERS. Death to the engine!
War on the tyrant Steam!

*JIMMY and NED LUD enter. The weavers turn to JIMMY
in alarm.*

NED LUD. A comrade born in Nottingham. For years a
traveller, now returned.

JIMMY greets the weavers.

NED LUD (*to* WIBLEY). Agreed?

WIBLEY. Agreed.

JIMMY comes forward.

JIMMY. On what?

JOHN WIBLEY. This very night we shall destroy the engine.

JIMMY, Madmen that you are!

JOHN WIBLEY. Are you another in the engine's pay?

JIMMY. Give me an hour to speak.

JOHN WIBLEY. Not half an hour remains.

NED LUD. Let him be heard.

JIMMY. Friends, you ran headlong when the spectre of this
engine raised his cruel head. Despair unmanned you. It
seemed a vampire stretching out its bloody claws to clutch
your souls. A god, a devil chaining you to drudgery. A
monster made to lame your bodies, blunt your minds, and
foul your honourable trade.

ALBERT. And so it is

JIMMY. There are other enemies, stronger than this frame of iron and wood they call an engine.

JOHN WIBLEY. He's making game of us!

CHARLES. Let him hold his tongue!

NED LUD. We gave him leave to speak.

JIMMY. An enemy lives in yourselves! He grips your minds. He swims in your life-blood. He has dulled and deadened the spirit in you.

JOHN WIBLEY. Oho, a parson!

CHARLES. See here, this is no church!

ALBERT. We are men, not women!

NED LUD. We must hear him out.

JIMMY. Brothers, look into yourselves! How joyless, how uneasy are your lives! Do you still know that there are forests? Dark, secret forests that awaken buried springs in men? Forests that quiver with stillness? Forests where men pray? Forests where men dance?

What is your trade to you? Are you weavers of your own free choice? Did you give yourselves to the task humbly and joyfully, like men who create? No! Your work was drudgery, wage-service, necessity.

Look into your children's faces! They are chalky, sickly. Boys of ten stumble like greybeards.

JOHN WIBLEY. Is poverty our fault?

JIMMY (*vehemently*). Your fault is that you gave in without a struggle, instead of standing shoulder to shoulder like a band of working brothers – instead of *living* for comradeship and bringing your stone, each of you, to build the house of justice!

Death is here among you! He crouches in your weary eyes. He burdens your heavy steps. He has killed your joy and laughter.

And yet dreams are in you! Dreams of wonderlands. Dreams of the world of justice, dreams of towns and countries and continents linked in common labour, each for all and all for each!

Brothers, join hands! Begin! Begin! Not I and I and I! No! World and we and thou and I! If you *will* the comradeship of workers, it is yours!

O, this winnowing will shake the chaff from your souls! The earth will sprout again! And the tyrant of machinery, conquered by your own creative spirit, will be your tool and your servant!

NED LUD. Our Tool . . .

JIMMY. What if you laboured to produce for all and not for Mammon – for service, not for gain? What if instead of sixteen hours you worked but eight? With the machine no more your enemy, but your helper! What if your children, freed from drudgery, grew up in sunny schoolrooms, gardens, playing fields?

Your misery holds you by the throat! Already you are well-nigh strangled. Be men and fight! Rouse yourselves! When leaves are rotten, let them dry, not moulder! Begin, brothers! Unite! Stand together and stand fast!

Silence.

JOHN WIBLEY. I hear words, words, words! Workmen unite – ha! We are outlaws: they slammed the doors of Parliament in our faces. Votes are not for us. Votes are for the money-bags!

JIMMY. We are for more than votes. Our land for our workers! England is ruled by her great lords; no room for rabble in their house. They make robber wars and call them wars for King and country. But who bleeds for their country? Is it Mammon?

WEAVERS. No, ourselves, ourselves!

JIMMY. We are preparing for the fight. In London we have founded a League that shall embrace every workman in the kingdom. In many towns already the beacon fire of resolution burns. The commonwealth shall be our master, not Mammon! Men shall rule, not machinery!

ARTHUR. Men – men – shall rule – not – not – machinery!

JIMMY. Are you ready to lend your brothers your right arm?

WEAVERS. We are! We are!

JIMMY. The fight is hard and calls for patience, brothers. It
will be harder than you guess. You must take service at the
engine. You must bear the old load for many a day – must
see your wives and children hunger, and hear yourselves
reproached and cursed!

WEAVERS. We are ready!

NED LUD. We choose you for our leader!

JIMMY. Each of you serves the people, each serves the cause.
Each of you our leader!

WEAVERS. Each serves the people, each serves the cause!

They lift JIMMY *on their shoulders and carry him out.*
JOHN WIBLEY *remains alone.*

JOHN WIBLEY. This vagabond Irishman carried shoulder
high! In scarce an hour he robs me of the leadership. And
these boobies would rule the earth and make it Paradise!
They may believe in it. Not I!

Curtain.

30

The Third Act

Scene One

A *room in* URE's *house.* HENRY COBBETT *alone, then*
JOHN WIBLEY.

HENRY. I sent for you. We'll make no mysteries with each
other. You know the new agitator?

JOHN WIBLEY. Yes, Mr Cobbett.

HENRY. You know his name?

JOHN WIBLEY. Jimmy Cobb –

HENRY. Well and good. They tell me you had words with
him. A difference of opinion, eh?

JOHN WIBLEY. Not that I know of –

HENRY. None of your acting here! I know the part you play.
Do you hear me? *I know the part you play* – every line of it.
There was no need to send for you, Wibley. It would have
been easier to have you fetched – in irons!

JOHN WIBLEY. You've got no proof –

HENRY. Come, we can save our breath in denials, both of us!
We have too much to lose. Cards on the table, Wibley! My
brother must leave Nottingham. Ure must not learn who the
agitator is. I give you twenty-four hours to get rid of him.
The time is short; the matter presses. You will be satisfied
with your pay.

JOHN WIBLEY. Cards on the table. Then I – I agree.

HENRY. Arrange it as you please; that's your affair.

JOHN WIBLEY. The game would be bold –

HENRY. Have you a plan?

JOHN WIBLEY. To wreck the engine after all – quietly to let

him know our plan – and then – then he would have to leave
the town –

HENRY. Your own affair. I play no part in it – you understand?

JOHN WIBLEY. Can I speak to Mr Ure?

HENRY. Is that necessary?

JOHN WIBLEY. Yes.

HENRY. Wait here.

He leaves the room.

JOHN WIBLEY (*alone*). Scum! Jack-in-office! Taskmaster,
overseer, driver maybe, but not the leader of a herd of
bellowing fools! This is an evening in a thousand. The door
is opened. – Pray step in, Mr Wibley. – Am I not cleverer
than that toady Cobbett? Nature has given me the fawning
hump. – Your most obedient servant, Mr Ure. Just as you
think fit, Mr Ure. – I throw myself at your feet, good Mr
Ure. We need lower wages, longer working hours? I'm
entirely of your opinion, Mr Ure. – But I'll make the cursed
pack laugh the wrong side of their mouths, trust me for that!
One milestone passed, but there are more to come. – Let me
but put a cushion to my back, for it stands in need of
fattening.

URE *enters.*

URE. John Wibley, weaver?

JOHN WIBLEY. Your servant, Mr Ure.

URE. Out of work?

JOHN WIBLEY. I was twelve years a weaver in your factory,
sir –

URE. I can take no account of individual claims. Industry is a
national interest. We must all bow to its requirements, I as
well as you.

JOHN WIBLEY. It's not work I'm after, Mr Ure.

URE. What then?

JOHN WIBLEY. I came because – because it goes against the

grain to see trouble made among the hands – because I have eaten my bread at your table these twelve years, Mr Ure.

URE. Come to the point. What is happening?

JOHN WIBLEY. There's a plot, Mr Ure, – a plot to destroy the engine.

URE. Take a seat, if you please. A cigar? Be good enough to give me all the details.

JOHN WIBLEY. An agitator from London has come to Nottingham. No one knows his name. A Communist. A member of the secret workers' league, and in the pay of France. He has been stirring up the weavers to destroy machinery. He promised them arms; said blood must flow.

URE. So there's a limit even you refuse to overstep. I'm glad of that, Wibley. The living blood of comradeship between master and man is no legend. I knew it. Labour makes us one.

JOHN WIBLEY. I will carry out your orders, Mr Ure.

URE (*slowly*). H'm. There is little to say at the moment. An attack on the engine will not alarm me. Rather the contrary. At a time like the present the actual occurrence of such a crime might well strengthen our position. It would open the eyes of our go-as-you-please Government, The material loss would be made good by the prospect of an orderly and well-regulated future. H'm. You understand me? I wish to be informed of every development that takes place.

JOHN WIBLEY. Very good, Mr Ure.

URE (*takes a sheet of paper and writes*). Give that to the cashier.

JOHN WIBLEY. Very good, Mr Ure.

URE'S *little daughter runs into the room, and clings to her father's knees.*

URE. Yes, Wibley, they talk of a gulf between master and man. Fiddlesticks! Take a father's love, for instance. What difference is there? When our children are sick we feel their pain as if it were our own. You as well as I. Good day to you, Wibley.

URE *and the little girl go out.*

JOHN WIBLEY (*alone*). Bloodsucker! The one famishes, the other starves him. Is that a difference? One child vomits in the lap of plenty, the other never sees white bread. Is that a difference? Scum, all of you, scum! And if you think, Master Ure, that I came creeping to your money-bags like a louse to your belly – bah! Call me a traitor! Fiddle-faddle! The ferret drives the polecat from the pigeon-loft. A change of tenants, nothing more. A traitor – ha! The word's a bogey fit to frighten children! A traitor? That depends on the result.

The stage is darkened.

Scene Two

A dirty street in front of JOHN WIBLEY*'s cottage. The houses are mostly one-storied.* JIMMY COBBETT *and* JOHN WIBLEY *meet.*

JIMMY. Blacklegs are working in the factory.

JOHN WIBLEY. I know.

JIMMY. But that must stop.

JOHN WIBLEY. 'Twas you preached patience to the men. You counselled work at the machines. You are to treat with Ure to-day. Ask him to send his interlopers home!

JIMMY. You wonder why I am resolved to treat with Ure? I'll tell you. This is not the hour for the decisive fight. We must avoid it. If we are driven to fight to-day, defeat is certain, and our strength will be exhausted. The hour will come when England will be ready. Then, comrade, there will be an end of bargaining! But now, *because* we treat with Ure, no other men must work. We must place pickets at the factory gates.

JOHN WIBLEY. Better to set upon the blacklegs in the shed, and hunt them home like rats – those that are fit to run!

JIMMY. Why set upon them, when persuasion serves our end? They are workmen like ourselves. Blind and misled, but workmen.

JOHN WIBLEY. We must have deeds, not words!

JIMMY. Is every deed an altar where men's knees must bow? A senseless deed makes fools drunk and cowards brazen.

JOHN WIBLEY. We need defeat. Rebels are bred in misery. Give them their bellyful and they spit on your counsel and turn to wallow in the trough like full-fed sows.

JIMMY. Rebels are bred in misery. But let the misery grow until it clutches every throat – till all are roofless, homeless, famishing. Are they good rebels then? Ask them for comradeship and they will scoff at you. Ask them to keep faith, and they will run to every trickster who lends the magic of words to their desires. Ask them for sacrifice, and they will be the hirelings and the prey of every leader who dangles the hope of booty before their greedy eyes.

JOHN WIBLEY. Hunt them from their lairs like wild beasts! Blood is the lash to whip them out of sloth!

JIMMY. With what contempt you speak of these workmen you would lead to freedom! What smouldering malice in your eyes! One would think you had no wish to free them, but only to revenge yourself! The man who arouses the baser instincts of the masses is overwhelmed by their fury; To-day he lets loose the storm, to-day he is a leader, to-morrow he is crushed by an avalanche of blind, mad passions, to-morrow he is a traitor spat upon by thousands!

JOHN WIBLEY. I've no book-learning, but we shall see who knows the workmen best. The working folk feel otherwise, think otherwise than you . . . : So we are to assemble at the factory-gate before the midday shift?

JIMMY. That would be best.

JOHN WIBLEY. There is no time to summon all the comrades for to-day.

JIMMY. It seems to me –

JOHN WIBLEY. Impossible. We must have time. I will summon all our friends to meet before the gate tomorrow night. Then we shall see how long the working folk will march with you.

JOHN WIBLEY *goes.* OLD REAPER *comes* out *of the house.*

OLD REAPER. Have you a minute to spare for me Jimmy? These eighty years my life has lasted now – and it was none of the best, for all the toil and trouble. Old Reaper has no wish to rise again when he is buried. He would grow into the earth – English meadow earth – so that flowers take root in his lap, and sheep nibble at his grass, beside a spring that dances merrily as a young he-goat. But before they lay Old Reaper in the grave let him ask you one thing: why this life, Jimmy? Where is the sense and purpose of it all?

JIMMY. Do you know why the tree grows, and puts out leaves that wither in the autumn? You ask for sense and purpose? I am, thou art, we are. That is the end of wisdom. Sense is given to life by men.

OLD REAPER. Do you believe in the kingdom of God? The Kingdom of Peace?

JIMMY. I fight as though I did.

OLD REAPER. Then tell me, where shall I find God?

JIMMY. I've never fallen in with Him. Maybe you'll find Him in yourself.

OLD REAPER. But aren't you fighting against God?

JIMMY. I fight as though I believed in Him.

OLD REAPER. He, he, he! The man's cracked! He fights against the engine, and doesn't know where God is! Your wits have gone a wool-gathering, Jim. You'll come to no good end.

JIMMY *smiles and goes away. A man with a four-wheeled barrow comes along the street.*

OLD REAPER. Hey! Man With the barrow, tell me, where shall I find God? I'll give you a hand with your barrow.

MAN WITH THE BARROW (*wrathfully*). I'm no man! I'm an
    official, I would have you know, and scavenger to the town
    of Nottingham. This is no barrow. A barrow has only two
    wheels. This is a four-wheeled cart. All my life I pushed a
    barrow. At last they've given me a cart. And now you call
    my cart a barrow!

OLD REAPER. It's not your barrow that we speak of, friend,
    but God.

MAN WITH THE BARROW. God doesn't bother me. Seek
    and you will find Him. We're talking of my cart you call a
    barrow. A barrow! A barrow, a barrow, he calls my
    four-wheeled cart.

OLD REAPER. I wanted to give you a hand with it.

MAN WITH THE BARROW. A fine helper indeed! A man
    who grudges another his advancement! Barrow, barrow,
    barrow! You'll call my cart an engine next!

OLD REAPER. The engine! But that's what I'm looking for!
    That's what I'm looking for!

The MAN WITH THE BARROW *goes away. A* BLIND
MAN, *led by a* DEAF AND DUMB MAN, *comes along
the street.*

Hey, brother blind man, where shall I find God?

BLIND MAN. I don't hear Him. Ask the man who leads me.

OLD REAPER. Hey, brother, tell me where shall I find God?

The DEAF AND DUMB MAN *makes signs that he does not
understand. The* BLIND MAN *laughs.*

What are you cackling at?

BLIND MAN. He, ha! He's deaf and dumb and doesn't see
    Him!

OLD REAPER. The blind man can't hear Him, the deaf and
    dumb man can't see Him. I have two good eyes and ears, but
    can't find Him.

The stage is darkened.

Scene Three

A square in front of URE's *house. A high wall encloses the garden. The main gate is in the middle, and a little wicket at the side. Children pass.*

FIRST BOY. I've seen the engine!

FIRST GIRL. So have I!

SECOND BOY. And I!

FIRST BOY. All shining, just like gold!

SECOND GIRL. Perhaps 'twas God that sent it.

FIRST BOY. Stupid!

SECOND GIRL. But parson says the angels brought it down.

FIR5T BOY. When you have played the blackleg for a day and night, then you may say 'Thank you, kind God!'

SECOND BOY. The old loom is a miserable thing.

SECOND GIRL. I like the engine best.

THIRD BOY. Let's hide. If father sees me, I am for the loom.

FIRST BOY. We're out on strike. You needn't weave to-day.

THIRD BOY. Shall I tell you a secret? My father's working.

FIRST GIRL. And mine!

FIRST BOY. These men don't hold together – shame on them!

The children run off. A procession of ragged women comes along.

WOMEN. We want no engine! We want no engine!

Silence.

FIRST WOMAN. Silent as blocks of wood they sit. Their door would open sooner to a yelping cur. I had to sell my last stick from the house. A bed, to pay the grocer. In that bed slept son and prentice, grandad, husband and myself. Many's the night I haven't known which took me in his arms. Now that last stick is gone.

SECOND WOMAN. Hey, masters, hey! Give us an answer! We are no robbers come to steal your goods by night. We are beggars – only beggars!

Silence. HENRY COBBETT *comes out of the house.*

WOMEN. We want no engine! We want no engine!

HENRY. The engine stands and waits for you. Give up your senseless strike and you have bread to-morrow. I have cheap hands enough – and none of them are shirkers.

WOMEN. Will all of us be taken on again?

HENRY. I grieve to say most of the men must be paid off. But all your children will be taken on. Children of three and four years old as well. And nimble girls. Be sensible, you women! The work demands deft fingers and a delicate touch.

FIR5T WOMAN. Sir, good sir, send the engine from the town. Your doves have grain, no roebuck starves. You feed the sparrows in the winter time, you build the sheep a fold. We are but men and women, sir, but have compassion, for Christ's sake. We cannot live if none but girls and women work. The devil tempted you, and sent you the machine. Sir, good sir, send the engine from the town!

WOMEN. Sir, good sir, send the engine from the town!

HENRY. We do our duty to our country. 'Tis true machinery displaces men, but only for a time. Why? I will tell you. We shall produce more goods in larger factories, at half the price. At half the price! Mark that, and listen. I will tell you what it means. To-day, for instance, you must pay four shillings to the parson for a burial. Six shillings more for a good plot of earth, say two yards long by one yard wide. Now suppose there came a joyful day when parson asked two shillings only, and the plot of earth were sold for three! Would you not die the easier for the thought of three days' wages saved to those you left behind? Half a week's wages! As eagerly as you would jump into the cheaper grave, the buyers run to purchase cheaper goods. Next comes a broadening of business and increase of demand. Give us goods! shout our customers. Goods! whistle the sirens of

the ships. Goods! rattle the waggons. Goods! Goods!
Goods! The end is that the factories grow out-of-date. New
factories, powerful factories, giant factories, spring up; their
doors are opened to the hungry workers. There are not hungry
men enough in England to feed those great factories – to
cram their gaping jaws, to fill their eager throats. Be patient,
women. Wait awhile! I would advise those men who find no
work today to go back to the land. If we could change the
world, good women, we would do it. But there are no
markets for the moment. Since the Great War, all Europe
has been crippled by a load of debt. You are Englishwomen,
you are patriots, you must know we cannot lend to bankrupt
debtors Our credit is our life. Our country first!

HENRY *goes back into the house. A silence of*
consternation.

LONG-DRAWN CRY OF THE WOMEN. Down with the
machines! (*A silence.*) Down with the machines!

MARY *comes stealthily out of the garden door. She pauses,*
startled, then makes as if to run away. Several women run to
her and drag her forward. They speak in rapid succession.

MARGARET. Where have you been?

SECOND WOMAN. Playing our husbands false in Cobbett's
bed.

THIRD WOMAN. Her nest's well feathered!

FOURTH WOMAN. So you would play the whore in master's
beds, while we stand here and beg – beg for a mouthful!

SECOND WOMAN *rushes at* MARY.

SECOND WOMAN. We'll tear out the pretty toy! We'll spoil
her beauty for her!

FOURTH WOMAN. The whip! the whip for hussies!

FIRST WOMAN. Tie her naked to a ladder! Let the children
spit upon her face!

SECOND WOMAN (*with a laugh*). She likes it warm!

MARGARET. A workman was too rough, too common for her!

WOMEN (*beating* MARY). You strumpet! Brazen slut! You
mattress-mopsy!

NED LUD *comes.*

NED LUD. John Wibley's wife? Are you wild beasts? Stand
back! Why are you beating her?

FIRST WOMAN. You're welcome, Lud. The woman's rotten
bad,
Worse than the creatures in the public stews.
We women starve. These seven weeks and more
Not one warm sup between us. We assemble,
We drag our swooning limbs to Cobbett's gate
And cry for riddance from machinery.

FOURTH WOMAN. Were you a woman, Ned Lud, you would
know
How hard it goes to bear a child, and then
With folded arms to see it starve and die!
A mother's agony!

MARGARET.   What man knows that!

FIRST WOMAN. Our misery, our pain, our aching care!

THIRD WOMAN. It seems to me Ure's wife should feel for us.

SECOND WOMAN. Ure's wife, ha, ha! When she's in need of
help
They call the midwife. For a pound or so
The bubble's pricked.

MARGARET. This hireling Cobbett told us to our face
The engine stays in Nottingham. The men
And older women, most of them, must go,
He drove us from the door like outworn dogs
And lay with her, a workman's wife, whose man
He throws into the gutter!

The women crowd in on MARY.

WOMEN. Beat the whore!

NED LUD (*pushing them back*). What, beat a child for
pouncing on a crust?
We are all famished. Mary, why were you there?

MARY (*in a low voice*). I am – so poor – I am like all the rest.
'Tis true I did it – but not for myself.

NED LUD. You fell upon this woman like wild cats.
Think with your heads for once, not with your bowels!
Had you her looks, you all would do as much.
You all have done it, too, when you were young.
Come, Mary, they'll not harm you. This way home.
(*To the* FIRST WOMAN). Come to me when your senses
have return'd.

NED LUD *and* MARY *go off.*

SECOND WOMAN. The devil take her!

CRIES. Death to the engine! Down with the thieving
shopkeepers! Blood or bread! Death to the engine!

The women form a procession and go off singing.

SONG.
Down, down, down and down,
Pauper and drudge and slave!
From moor and meadow, street and loom,
From sty and dunghill, hutch and tomb,
Hark to the thunder call of doom,
Work or the grave!

During the scene OLD REAPER *has come.*

OLD REAPER. They shall cast their silver in the streets, and
their gold shall be removed; their silver and their gold shall
not be able to deliver them in the day of the wrath of the
Lord; they shall not satisfy their souls, neither fill their
bowels; because it is the stumbling block of their iniquity.
If I were He, I would let manna fall from heaven. But He
makes no sign. When will He stir? When trumpets blow and
golden harps greet kings and conquerors? The poor have no
such music. Their moan is softer than the heart-beat of a
child. You must have good ears to hear it. You must listen
close to unwashed bosoms, stinking bosoms to hear it. I will
cheer the womenfolk a little.

OLD REAPER *takes a stick, and makes as if to play a
violin. Two women pass.*

FIRST WOMAN. Look at the cracked old man!

OLD REAPER (*as if speaking to many dancing women*). What, are you blown already? I've played three steps, no more. What do you say? You have no legs for dancing? You can scarcely stand? You are to dance and you can – scarcely – stand? Aye, aye, to be sure. Aye, aye, to be sure.

Curtain.

The Fourth Act

Scene One

A room in URE's *house.* HENRY COBBETT *is writing at a high desk. Muffled sounds are heard from the Factory, and sirens whistle. Enter* JIMMY COBBETT.

HENRY. You here? What do you want? Out of here this minute! Our porters carry dog-whips. The police know how to deal with ragged tramps. And the King's soldiers have a bullet in their pouch or a halter in their knapsack for the rebel!

JIMMY. Tell Mr Ure I want to see him, brother.

HENRY. Brother? I know of no brother.

JIMMY. Then tell him that a stranger waits.

HENRY. No!

JIMMY. Mr Ure's door is never closed to callers on important business. Am I to ask the servants to announce me?

HENRY. If you possess a spark of brotherly feeling, go! Leave Nottingham. England is wide. You will find dupes enough. Why must you be revenged on me? I used to beat you long ago when we were boys. Well – I was wrong.

JIMMY. So conscience stirs when your position is in danger?

HENRY. Oh, this is infamous! You have come back to wreak your spite on me!

JIMMY. One bosom gave us life. My word upon it, Henry, Ure will never hear my name or know whose brother speaks to him. And that you may sleep in peace o' nights, I promise you this as well. One week more, or two at most, I stay in Nottingham. Farewell, brother. Greet the old woman from me – say I know how hard it was for her –

HENRY. Here, take money. My month's salary. Go to-day –
   go now – this hour!

JIMMY. An English mother bore me. She taught me English
   speech. The horn-book where you learned the ABC of men
   is strange to me. Show me in, Henry. (*The other hesitates.*)
   Or must I knock?

HENRY. Good God, I'm ruined! If I lose my place, and mother
   starves, the curses of her dying hour be on your head!

He goes.

JIMMY (*alone*). And are *one* blood!

URE enters.

URE. Your name?

JIMMY. Call me Nameless. Or call me, if you will, the
   Full-timer, as you call your workmen full-timers or
   half-timers, when they man the looms as your submissive
   stock-in-trade.

URE. Your tone is impudent. I have no time for trifling. What
   do you want with me? On principle I never give to beggars.
   Try the vicar, my good man.

JIMMY. I may not be unknown to you. They call me the
   outlandish rebel who has taught the folk of Nottingham that
   workmen can be men.

URE. You dare?

JIMMY. I dare. The spirit owns no slavery,
   No bondage to the masters of this earth.
   The mind's eternal law, in adamant
   Chisell'd upon the welkin of mankind,
   Commands that men keep faith with what they know.
   The coward who quits his Thought betrays himself.
   I speak for thousands deaden'd by a yoke
   Of dull oppression – seeking for the word
   That shall translate the heart-beat of their soul.
   I say to you that no man has the right
   To rob another of that scanty bread
   Without which he must wither like mown grass.

You cry aloud that work alone can save us,
And turn your practis'd craftsmen out of doors!
While countless women lack a cotton shift
To cover them, you leave the bales to rot,
Dismiss your weavers, and abuse your power
To grind a niggard wage to nothingness.
Out of the cruel fountain-head of war
Still runs the heart-blood of a continent.
Want cries aloud in prisons of despair.
Here men go hungry, there the granaries
Are choked with mildew'd corn. Here is no coal,
The people freeze, and there, above the pits,
The coal stands mountain-high. If the demand
Is lacking, ask yourselves the reason why;
Yours is the system that will have it so.
 The market's at a standstill? Trade is bad?
You leave the masses scarce a pauper's dole
 And whimper 'Trade is bad.'
O, you are blind, and for your blindness' sake
It is our task to see this world aright.
Give work to workers! Thousands will have bread
If you but shorten hours. Consider well
Before you crush with wanton heel the lives
That, like your own, were pressed into this world
To march along the road of nameless fate
And meet their doom. 'Tis God who perishes
When you destroy a brother's livelihood.

URE. Who are you, sir?
Your dress bespeaks no quality of mind.
God and our business have no truck together.
God is the shield of lonely, silent men,
To Whom they look for succour in distress.
God is too good for daily bargainings
And earthly cares. God is the Lamp of truth,
The Light of mercy shining far above
All human need. We should profane His goodness
Were we to banish Him to household tasks.
What would you have? Our town was peaceable
Until you came. You threw the torch of anger
Into a witless flock of brutish men

Whom the State shepherds into quietude
With patient toil. What is your purpose, Sir?
Ruin? Are you an enemy of peace
Who never rests until revolt and bloodshed
Like a volcano pour their lava streams
On towns and villages, to set ablaze
The scaffolding of diligent endeavour?

JIMMY. Your hands they were that threw the torch of war
Into our marching ranks. 'Tis you who tear
The stragglers from the body of mankind,
So that they stand forlorn and may not look
Their brothers in the face, unless in hatred.
You make our earth an endless battlefield
Where strong men crush the weak, and artful men
Outwit the simple – where the dastard hires
A cut-throat for his bidding, where the dupes
Lie buried and the bloodstain'd conquerors
Are counted heroes.

URE. Young man, the dreams you dream are dangerous.
You walk this earth as blind men walk. Life grows
To manhood in the universal fray.
The stag supplants the rival at his hip
And sires a lusty race of antler'd kings.
The conqueror breeds his kind, and not the weakling!
The harmony of freedom takes its root
On the grim battlefield of interest.
He who survives, survives by Nature's law
Which must remain unfathom'd by our minds.
'Tis thus we ripen, thus we civilize.

JIMMY. O, let a foe molest the weaker stag
And you will see the stronger take his stand
Beside his brother, lending him his power!
You speak of freedom and of interest,
Of battles fought and won, of master-men
Who live as conquerors by Nature's law.
Freedom for all! you cry. What freedom has
The weaver in your service? He is free
To die, maybe, but not to live and labour.
How prosperous was once the lot of slaves!

Their lord was their protector, foster-father,
They were not left to freeze in pitiless streets!
How enviable was the lot of guildsmen
Who fashioned tower on tower by noble toil
In unison with their masters! And to-day?
Free men, we drag in chains a load of want
That throttles every vein of manly blood.
What are we? Wares! A Thing! A hated, hateful
Thing! From the wells of life as far removed
As that old loom from your great engine-shed!
Aye, look to Nature's law. Where lives the brute
That lives alone? The eagle soaring calmly
Espies his head of game. He gives a cry
To warn his neighbour eagles, and together
They swoop upon the field to share the prize.
The full-fed ant will vomit up his meal
To feed the hungry of the common clan.
The sexton-beetle calls the neighbours in
To burrow him a house for his unborn.
The negroes live in cheerful comradeship
With fellows of their tribe; where all are one
In blood, there all are bound in brotherhood.
None but free men of cultur'd lands are deaf
When THOU, and WE, and ONE ANOTHER call.

URE. 'Tis plain your words are felt. And you and I
Stand on that field where strong men's pride compels
The battle. There's the law we speak of.

JIMMY. Let me but name that natural law again.
Your law of Nature is the law of money!
Money lends mastery to the man who gives
Another work. Not mind, not rank, but money!
Your conquerors are not chosen, but impress'd,
Not garlanded, but coin'd! And you, the lords
Of money, sink to be its patient drudge!
Money is master! Money bids you crush
The Indian peoples, children of the Spring.
And money bids you spread destruction wide
Through Eastern wonderlands, with devil's brews
Of opium and brandy. Money bids you burn

The garner'd store of riper lands for gain.
O, what you name a virtue, Nature's law,
The strong man's birthright, is your deepest shame,
The bond of self-made slavery, the badge
Of an insatiate demon, urging you
From war to war!
To wars against your brothers of one blood,
To wars of nations, races, continents.
The universal fray indeed, a war
Against YOURSELVES!

URE. And you?

JIMMY.   Within our breast there is a bud
That longs to be unfolded, hiding wonder
On wonder in its petals. It is THOU!
That THOU can lift the Scriptural curse of toil,
And what is now our scourge, our brand of bondage
Shall be again our holy, happy task!

A silence.

URE. You dream. Yet I would have you dream beside me.
Henceforward you are welcome to my house.

JIMMY. Not so. Will you give work to workers, Sir?

URE (*resuming the official tone*). We must return to business,
since you wish it. The terms of work are known; I have no
more to add to them. They have been well considered.
Expediency, not sympathy, must be our guide in these
affairs.

JIMMY. We fight against you, and yet on your side.
For you, your child, and all your children's children,
The light of justice flames upon our banner!

JIMMY goes.

URE (*alone*). A fool. A strange fool. A sanguine fool. A
dangerous fool. A man!

HENRY enters.

HENRY. Sir?

URE. A man was here! (*Recollecting himself.*) He must be

watched, and sharply! Tell the police to keep an eye upon
him. Have you made all arrangements for the manning of
the engine?

HENRY. The last batch of hands has just arrived from Carlton.

URE. You may go.

The stage is darkened.

Scene Two

NED LUD'S *cellar, furnished with a table and stools. In the
background is a heap of straw on which children lie.*
MARGARET *and* NED LUD *sit at the table.* MARGARET
holds the youngest child in her arms, and sings a lullaby.

MARGARET. Hey, poppy, hey, poppy, moon, mine,
  Our good Lord will be here for you soon, mine,
  Pack you in a golden chest, O,
  Lay you in the grave to rest, O,
  Earth on you,
  Earth on me,
  Hand in hand we knock at Heaven's gate,
  Hand in hand we knock at Heaven's gate.

She lays the child in the straw, and returns to the table.

  What, the cash-box here? The hidden money? Not in my
  house, if you please!

NED LUD. My wife a swab! Leave me some comfort, Mag.

MARGARET. You are the same old fool as ever. Let John
  Wibley keep the money.

NED LUD. Are you afraid they'll rummage in our cellar?

MARGARET. I have nine children.

NED LUD. So have I, Mag. So have I.

MARGARET. Look at them. See the youngest boy. When
  I have bedded him in lousy straw, then – God forgive me –
  I could wish I'd laid him in the grave.

NED LUD. He was born ailing.

MARGARET. Is that my fault? Till the last hour of labour I
was standing at the loom. And then – what then? After three
days the foreman sent to ask if I should be at work next
morning. What could I do? At half-past four next morning I
was in the stifling mill. Wet weaving – linen-yarn it was. All
day the milk was running from my breasts. And how they
smarted! When I left the factory that night at nine, my
clothes were clinging to me from the milk. I was too tired to
eat a crust. 'Twas three o'clock before I came to bed.

NED LUD. Now, Mag, who's blaming you?

MARGARET. The blame . . . the blame . . . I think they crucify
Christ every day. God asks the murderers before His throne:
Where is thy brother Abel? When will He ask our masters
for a reckoning of men they starved, women and little ones
they left to die? God-fearing gentry that they call themselves
– they eat and drink, go whoring, eat and drink again. Their
bellies are our burden – pah!

NED LUD. An end will come of it, I say.

MARGARET. All brag!

NED LUD. I am an English workman, and don't lie.

MARGARET. Workmen are soldiers, gaolers, hangmen –
workmen all! 'Tis workmen build their gallows for them.
Pah! Your eyes are guns. Well, fire away! I'm not afraid.
This cash-box. Is it the money of the secret league?

NED LUD. So you would have me blab?

MARGARET. You tell me not a word, although I am your
wife. I'm good for bed, maybe. Or good to mind the brats.

NED LUD (*embracing her*). Well, there's a shrew! A
workman's wife, and wants her man to let his tongue run
loose.

MARGARET (*going*). Nine children are enough. Mark that!

NED LUD *alone. Then* YOUNG LUD *enters, drunk, and
arm- in-arm with a street walker.*

YOUNG LUD (*singing*).
  A bed of moss, a bed of straw,
  A bed for kings, a bed –

NED LUD. What's that?

YOUNG LUD. 'Evening to you, dad. My bride is brought to
  bed – ha, ha – I've brought my bride to –

NED LUD. Pack up!

YOUNG LUD. We will – into the straw. And close, I promise
  you.

NED LUD. Take that baggage out of here, I say!

YOUNG LUD. Would you insult my bride?

NED LUD. Be off, I say, or I'll lay hands on you!

YOUNG LUD. Oho, dad, that's your tune? And who's the
  breadwinner? Tell me that! How long have I been working
  for you at the mill? Since four years old! And who cared
  what became of me? Did you? Or mother? Who kept you
  from the streets, these many months? I did. And now you
  want to spoil an evening's sport.

NED LUD. Out, I say! Aren't you ashamed to look your
  mother in the face?

YOUNG LUD. Mother! Oho! She knew a thing or two when
  she was young. Like my bride here. Well, keep your straw!
  the woods will serve as well. But I give notice, dad; I mean
  to quit. No penny-piece do you get from me, from this day
  forward. So goodbye, old blockhead. (*Singing.*) A bed of
  straw, a bed of moss.

  YOUNG LUD *and his companion stagger out.* NED LUD
  sits down with his head in his hands. Enter JOHN WIBLEY.

NED LUD. You're welcome, John.

JOHN WIBLEY. Now there's a man who feels for working
  folk! Ned, you brought Mary home to-day. You brought –
  Mary – home.

NED LUD. Let be, John. Say no more. I am no parson. I know
  what poverty means.

JOHN WIBLEY. Their pleasure shall be paid for – yes, in bloody tears!

NED LUD. Our women have been plundering the bakers' shops.

JOHN WIBLEY. They have done well. Did you see Ure?

NED LUD. This morning.

JOHN WIBLEY. Well, what news?

NED LUD. None of the best.

JOHN WIBLEY. Will all of us be taken on again?

NED LUD. Seventy-five in every hundred men must go. And no more ailing women will be wanted. All the children will be taken on. We asked what workless men should do. Well, well, said Mr Ure, there was a hope, if trade looked up, of building bigger factories. Meanwhile the men had time to think of the next world. And he went on to say machinery called for suppleness, not strength. Our hands, he said, were too big-boned, too hard about the knuckle-joints, too stiff and heavy to be suited to the engine.

JOHN WIBLEY. Good, good. We are to think of our immortal souls. And rub our hands with oil, maybe, to make them supple. A fine plan indeed! What wages does he offer?

NED LUD. Fivepence for children. Eightpence for women, and a shilling for the men.

JOHN WIBLEY. And the conditions?

NED LUD. They are hard, John. We must bind ourselves for one year's service. Ure can dismiss a weaver on the nod for scanty work or breach of regulations. If we break spool or shuttle, brush or can, we have to pay for them. And the fines! They're bigger than the wage. A penny for forgetting scissors. Threepence for quitting place at the machine. Fivepence for going out without permission of the foreman. Fourpence for talking to your neighbour, singing, whistling. We must live in Ure's cottages, and take his goods for half our earnings.

JOHN WIBLEY. Good, good. He makes us pay our wages back again in fines and rents. And what does Jimmy say to that?

NED LUD. Jimmy's advice is to agree. He says the masters' days are numbered. In Blackburn, Bolton, Rochdale, Wigan, Derby, Manchester, the weavers are preparing. He says we must put off the fight till every town is ready.

A crowd of women presses in, among them MARGARET. The FIRST WOMAN throw loaves to the children out of her apron.

MARGARET. Here, children, fill your bellies. Seven lean years will come.

The children fall greedily on the bread.

NED LUD. Bread from the plundered shops! I won't allow it!

MARGARET. Ha, ha, he won't allow it! I could die of laughing! He won't allow it! The gentleman! The saint! Like chained-up dogs that fall upon a bone, your children gnaw their stolen crust. Well, take it from them, Ned! Now show your mettle. Take it from them – the stolen loaves – the bread of wickedness – ha, ha! What, tears! The man is crying. What do I see? The great Ned Lud, the man of iron, in tears!

Silence.

SECOND WOMAN. Is it true you counsel working at the engine?

NED LUD. It's true.

FIRST WOMAN. And that the men are bargaining with Ure?

NED LUD. We must have justice done to all. The engine's not our enemy.

FIRST WOMAN. What does that mean?

SECOND WOMAN. Can't you see? They leave us in the lurch.

JOHN WIBLEY. If you must have it so. We leave you in the lurch.

FIRST WOMAN. Ha, ha! And what of justice? We're for justice, too. And we'll not work for engines. Never, never!

JOHN WIBLEY. You must do it, for our sakes.

MARGARET. John Wibley! Wibley snivelling like a parson! Have none of you got marrow in your bones?

FIRST WOMAN. You hamstrung shufflers! Who would sleep a night with you?

NED LUD. Why do you rage? You women will be taken on. Ours is the hardest lot.

FIRST WOMAN. Oh, you can sweep the rooms, and cook the dinner, darn the socks. A noble trade for men!

NED LUD. And if you snap your fingers at Ure's terms, your children starve!

MARGARET. Then let them starve! I would they were unborn. Shall we have time for children now? Scarce time enough to suckle them. They'll grow up like a cuckoo-brood. We'll have to farm them out. Family! Mother-love! O, they do well to talk, our masters! What have our like to do with home and family? The weaving-stool is more to me than my own child. What do I know of children? That they cry for food!

FIRST WOMAN. Get our husbands bread, we say! Else we, the wives, will make a league against you!

JOHN WIBLEY. What would you do?

FIRST WOMAN. What would we do? Why, go to Ure and beg him to take women on in place of the remaining men. Try us and see. We have the hands for weaving. We can work for twenty hours a day, if need be. And for half your wages.

NED LUD. For shame! Would you betray your brothers and your trade?

FIRST WOMAN. Our trade – ha, ha! When our children eat the grass of poverty, are we to sing them lullabies of trade and brothers? Good brothers, save us!

SECOND WOMAN. We must have deeds.

NED LUD. Hear what Jimmy says: Jimmy means well by us. He speaks our mind; he tells us what we feel. Here, John, I am no talker, as you know. Tell them what Jimmy said to us.

JOHN WIBLEY. From boyhood's days I always fell asleep at sermon-time. 'Twas so with me last night. I'll not compare old parson's discourse with the sermon Jimmy gave us. But I woke when all was over.

SECOND WOMAN. We are no men, to hang upon the lips of vagabond preachers!

FIRST WOMAN. We give you two days'_grace, you flabby-guts!

The women go.

JOHN WIBLEY. But Jimmy says we must submit.

NED LUD. Only no treachery! We must stand united. Else we are blades that bend to every breeze. Our strength is in the mass.

JOHN WIBLEY. Do you know that Ure has brought two hundred unemployed from Carlton? They're working in the factory.

NED LUD. The scabs!

JOHN WIBLEY. I spoke with Jimmy on the matter.

NED LUD. And what did he advise?

JOHN WIBLEY. Patience.

NED LUD. Patience! That can't be!

JOHN WIBLEY. Jimmy knows nothing of a workman's pride. He is no workman, though he takes our part. Why, he can read and write like gentlefolks!

NED LUD. We must defend ourselves!

JOHN WIBLEY. Aye, so say all the rest. To-night we gather by the smaller shed. We'll notch a score or two of black sheep, never fear!

NED LUD. To-night, you say?

JOHN WIBLEY. At nine o'clock.

NED LUD. I shall be there.

JOHN WIBLEY. Whatever Jimmy says?

NED LUD. My name's Ned Lud. Are all the comrades warned?

JOHN WIBLEY. All except Bobby. I must see him now. (*At the door.*) I met one of Ure's book-keepers. He told me Jimmy's always in and out there. He even said 'twas Jimmy counselled Ure to bring the men from Carlton. But that I don't believe.

JOHN WIBLEY goes out. NED LUD and MARGARET remain. A silence.

MARGARET. It seems a spell is on us, since the engine came to town. But there was sense in what the women said.

NED LUD (*angrily*). Margaret!

MARGARET. Flabby-guts you are! You pray with pious faces while your womenfolk and children perish. Ned Lud will empty slops. I'll give you an old petticoat. Here, pull it on and grin!

A child's cry is heard. She runs to the straw.

The babe! The babe! O, God in Heaven, my babe is in a fit! He's dead!

NED LUD. Stock still we stand, while heavy things spin round us. There's the machine – and there – and there – How clear all seemed while Jimmy spoke! And now – Back to the soil were best for us. The city runs like poison in our veins. Townsmen break faith. We must have earth again. So we should have a homeland. We are like the lepers. Like trees whose roots are cut. They stand against the storm, and yet they wither.

Curtain.

The Fifth Act

Scene One

A street in Nottingham, at dusk. The shapes of the houses are blurred. The scene passes like a ghostly flicker.

JOHN WIBLEY. In two hours' time. Why do you start?

ALBERT (*with a shiver*). The engine!

JOHN WIBLEY. Jimmy is in the masters' pay.

ALBERT. It was the engine bought him!

JOHN WIBLEY. Albert, what if we did more than hunt the blacklegs out? What if we took up the fight against our enemy, the engine?

ALBERT. That would save us! That would save us!

JOHN WIBLEY. You're with us, then?

ALBERT. To the last drop of blood. But Jimmy's cast a spell upon the men.

JOHN WIBLEY. Ha, ha! Fine words that warmed their cockles for a night! Already they are muttering at Ure's terms. Already they are asking whether Jimmy's hands are clean. Already they are whispering tales of snares and pitfalls. Let them but look the engine in the face, and Jimmy's counsel will be blown away like chaff! The women do their part. See to the women, Albert; ply them well! Jimmy will not be in the mill to-night. He thinks we meet to-morrow.

ALBERT. The women, first to shout and first to run! But Ned Lud's different. I'd a dog once that set his teeth in a goat's neck. I had to beat him dead before he loosed his hold. Ned Lud is such a man.

JOHN WIBLEY. Do you know Henry Cobbett is Jimmy's brother?

ALBERT. You told me that. But Jimmy has no truck with home.

JOHN WIBLEY. No matter. We shall gain Ned Lud. And if Ned Lud stands in with us, then, Jimmy, watch yourself!

ALBERT (*crying out*). O God!

JOHN WIBLEY. What's to do?

ALBERT (*terror-struck*). There's some one near us listening. The engine's near us!

JOHN WIBLEY. You give a man the creeps. Befriend me, night! We shall win through.

The stage is darkened.

Scene Two

An old potato shed, with straw on the floor. JIMMY *sits on the straw, writing. The* BEGGAR *comes in.*

BEGGAR. So you are there?

JIMMY. Why, are they looking for me?

BEGGAR. No, friend. Just the other way about.

JIMMY. The other way about?

BEGGAR. The seekers have gone dancing.

JIMMY. None of your riddles!

BEGGAR. What are you doing there?

JIMMY. Writing a pamphlet.

BEGGAR. Pamphlets – drifting sand. They stop the eyes and ears, but go no deeper. Say, friend, are you sure of your men?

JIMMY. They are working men.

BEGGAR. No less men for that.

JIMMY. Working men keep faith

BEGGAR. Some of them, maybe. But all? There's a question.
Do all men keep their word, are all men brave and true? No.
Then why working men? Because they work? Look at them
as they are, and not as you would have them be. These are
your new gods, called 'holy workmen.' True gods, pure
gods, wise gods, perfect gods – English weavers of 1815.
Aye, so you dream. My friend, the man who fights with
gods for comrades will ride to victory as surely as an
apple-blossom comes to fruit. Open your eyes and see that
they are only men, good and bad, greedy and generous, petty
and great-hearted – and yet try your luck with them. If you
win through and they change their nature in the fight, I take
off my hat to you. Always providing that I have a hat. For
yours is gone. It was drowned. It lies in a warm place. If you
refuse to see men as they are, never speak to me of treachery
or ingratitude.

JIMMY. The workers fight for justice.

BEGGAR. I have lived under three governments. All
governments cheat the people, some more, others less.
Those that cheat them least are called good governments.

JIMMY. You're a Jeremiah.

BEGGAR. Jimmy, you're an educated workman. That means
an aristocrat. All aristocrats have the itch to rule. And
workmen, too, have their aristocrats. Now don't jump down
my throat, friend. For if you have the itch to rule, you may
be one of those who do it well. Aye, very well.

JIMMY (*laughs. After a silence*). Do you know John Wibley?

BEGGAR. Wibley with the hump?

JIMMY. John Wibley.

BEGGAR. His father drank me under the table. And that's no
small matter. When he came home drunk he used to beat his
wife and children. One night he threw John against the wall
as you might throw a cat. The boy lay where he fell. When
he came to his feet he was a cripple. The mother hanged
herself because she had stolen a loaf from the baker's, and
stood in fear of being jailed. The baker said she took three
loaves, but we know the bakers. They say they bake rye
bread, but the rye often stinks of powdered alum.

JIMMY. Do the weavers look up to John Wibley?

BEGGAR. He can be masterful.

JIMMY. What does that mean?

BEGGAR. O, he can rule the roost, has a good pair of jaws,
and threw a stone once at the manager's back – but that was
after dark.

JIMMY. And is his boy a cripple?

BEGGAR. No more than other weavers' children. The
midwives say they hardly know whether the newborn babes
have bones. They feel like rubber.

JIMMY. If we could but save the children! This future
generation eaten to the marrow!

A silence.

BEGGAR. And you would lead men! Let me laugh! Run to the
vicar; get him to make you colonel of a regiment of angels!
This man would lead others, and can't see what is happening
under his nose!

JIMMY. What is happening?

BEGGAR. Why, man, the mares are calving, the rose-bushes
are sprouting lilies, and men and women crying 'Halleluia,
our new prophet!'

JIMMY. What does that mean?

BEGGAR. Halleluia, new prophet!

JIMMY. Answer me!

BEGGAR. Halleluia, new prophet! (*He sets a plaited wreath of
straw on* JIMMY's *head.*) All hail!

JIMMY. Away with your trash!

BEGGAR (*suddenly*). Hush! Do you hear?

JIMMY. I hear nothing.

BEGGAR. Put your head in the straw and listen.

JIMMY. I hear a rustling.

BEGGAR. Hush!

JIMMY. Yes, it rustles.

BEGGAR. Man, you sit on a volcano and say 'It rustles.' It crashes! It thunders! It flashes fire, it blazes brimstone, it bubbles murder. Says the great leader, 'It rustles.'

JIMMY. Are you crazed?

BEGGAR (*imitating the sound of marching men*). Tramp, tramp, tramp, tramp, tramp, tramp.

JIMMY. A drop too much.

BEGGAR. Tramp, tramp, tramp, tramp!

JIMMY. The taverns should be closed –

BEGGAR. And babes in arms should not be breeched too soon –

JIMMY. Or dotards given a rattle –

BEGGAR. To whimper over the ingratitude of men.

JIMMY. You're hiding something from me?

BEGGAR. So you're awake at last! Up with you, Jimmy! To-night your workmen smash the engine.

JIMMY. You lie!

BEGGAR. John Wibley is their leader.

JIMMY. It is false!

BEGGAR. Be off with you to London, man from cloud-land, before they do to you what they are doing to King Steam!

JIMMY. Where – where shall I find them?

BEGGAR. Why, at his Court.

JIMMY. Farewell –

BEGGAR (*calling after him*). Take care, my friend; take care! If they lose belief in you, they'll hang you. If they feel they're in the wrong, they'll hang you first. You've forgotten your crown, Jimmy! And your shirt too! May I keep it? He's out of hearing. These men who would conquer the world, with gods to help them! I'll take the shirt for luck. It's two years since I wore one. The man who wears a shirt feels a lord. But the man who wears none, and has a pint of liquor in him, feels a king. I'll have no truck with lordship when a kingdom beckons. Sir innkeeper, I confer this shirt upon thee, and make thee my cupbearer. Why, even a lord would scratch himself, if he lived in this palace.

The stage is darkened.

Scene Three

The factory by moonlight, with a gigantic steam engine and mechanical looms, at which children and a few women are seated. Beside the engine are two men. Amid the sounds of machinery are heard the hum of the transmitters, the clear tone of the running crankshafts, the deep rumble of the levers, and the regular whirr and rattle of the shuttles. Stokers tend the furnace.

HENRY (*as Overseer*). Nine o'clock gone! All hands to work! (*To a little girl.*) You there! Do you hear me?

LITTLE GIRL. I can never sleep in daytime, sir – and now I can scarcely keep my eyes open –

HENRY *strikes her with a strap. She seats herself and goes on with her work. A boy comes on.*

HENRY. Two minutes past the hour. Two minutes late for work. There's twopence off your earnings. Set about it! (*Boy goes to his place. A pause.*) Doors closed! (*A woman shuts the door. Knocking.*) Who's there?

VOICE. Mary Anne Walkley.

HENRY. Twelve minutes past the hour, by factory time. The doors are closed at ten past. You wait until the next shift starts at one o'clock. It will be entered in your punishment book. You lose half a day's wages.

VOICE. O, sir, I was unwell to-day –

HENRY. That's no concern of mine. The regulations are my business. Paragraph One of standing orders! (*Steps are heard going away; then fresh knocking.*) Who's there?

VOICE. Ure!

HENRY (*obsequious*). Very good, sir. Directly, sir.

He opens. URE *enters with his guest, a Government representative.*

URE. All in order?

HENRY. Quite in order, sir.

URE. Are all the hands full-timers?

HENRY. Yes, sir. All of them, sir.

URE (*to his guest*). Here you see the factory. Agents of our foreign rivals nickname it 'the house of dread' or 'the shambles'; but agitators love strong language. It's true machinery disciplines the rebel hand; for that we may be grateful . . . Look at the children, my dear sir. Do you see any signs of weariness, ill-usage, discontent? How their eyes sparkle! How they enjoy the light play of their muscles! How they revel in the natural suppleness of youth! Ah, they have life before them! How charming the nimble movement with which this little girl ties up a broken thread! How all of them rejoice to show their skill before my guest! An artist's satisfaction, is it not?

GUEST. And yet one hears it said that children's wages are too low.

URE. The claptrap of the theorists, my dear sir. Wages *must* be low. Low wages are the manufacturer's only defence against the parent's greed. Believe me, they would send their sucklings to the mill if we would let them. There are no greater sharks than working parents. They batten on their children's health and strength.

GUEST. But are not night-shifts harmful to the children's health?

URE. Not in the least. Besides, we have no choice; the competition is too keen. If we dispensed with night-shifts the mills would soon be altogether idle.

GUEST. Parliament proposes to limit child labour to thirteen hours a day.

URE. Parliament, my dear sir, Parliament! Such legislation means an end to freedom. We must allow the worker liberty to choose his hours.

GUEST. And have the children intervals for meals?

URE. To our sincere regret we are unable to make this concession. The furnaces, you see, have to be stoked continually. The waste of coal would be criminal.

GUEST. And is the overseer an ex-workman?

URE. Yes, an ex-workman. We must make way for the man with brains, provided he is honest, obedient, hard-working, sound in wind and limb. We have always found that ex-workmen give the best results as overseers. They soon throw off all relationship to their former fellows. They are assimilated, so to speak. We find them reliable and unyielding in their strictness – the very best of servants.

GUEST. An uplifting reflection. And when do you think this foolish strike will be abandoned?

URE. The end may come at any moment. We have hands enough at our disposal – unemployed weavers from Carlton and orphan children from the poorhouse, who are used to the machine. But a senseless spirit of rebellion is abroad among our lower orders. The dangerous, romantic moonshine of English liberalism, fostered by vain and work-shy scribblers. We want to do our best for all our hands. They too are Christians. That is not to be forgotten. We are but human. And our reward? Our reward is ingratitude, my dear sir. Come!

URE *and his guest leave the factory.*

HENRY. Get on with your work, and quit staring! (*To a boy.*) You whistled something. What's your tune?

BOY. Britons never shall be slaves.

HENRY. Your name goes down in the punishment book. A penny fine. What do I see? Hey! (*He goes to a stool where a little girl has fallen asleep, huddled up.*) This sinful world! The creature goes to sleep at work! Hey!

He shakes her roughly. The girl wakes with a start and goes on weaving mechanically. Loud knocking at the door.

THE ENGINEER (*outside*). Open, open! (*He is admitted.*) A mob of weavers armed with picks and shovels – at the factory gate –

HENRY. All keep your places at the loom! (*To a child.*) Run to the Town Hall, you.

The child slips out. The shouts of the mob are heard as they approach. Knocking, then banging, on the door.

CRIES. Open! Open!

The door is forced. Among the mob who break into the shed are NED LUD, JOHN WIBLEY, CHARLES, GEORGE, EDWARD, ALBERT, ARTHUR.

CRIES. Scabs, all of you! To hell with blacklegs! Down with the Judas overseer!

The women and children from the looms shrink away into a corner.

CRIES. Why, they're children!

ALL. Children!

A CRY. Look at the iron man!

The mob see the engine. They are overwhelmed by wonder and stand transfixed. There is a sudden silence.

NED LUD. So grind the mills of God, maybe!

HENRY. Engineer! Engineer! Good God, my place is lost!

ENGINEER. Stop working! Shut off steam!

The engine stops. He leaps on to the bridge.

What would you do,
You simpletons? Fly out at Providence?
You trod the looms like galley-slaves, with limbs
Bent crooked by the load of drudgery.
The engine's your salvation! Even now
The boiler quivers on the glowing coals,
Pregnant with steam! One touch is all it needs!
The engine quickens! Energy is born!

*He pulls a lever. With a sound like a human sigh the
machinery begins to work.*

The fly-wheels waken, stretch themselves,
Whirl in a humming melody!
The sliding pulleys tug their belts.
One touch! the frame of yarn is warp'd,
Another, and the weft is thrown!
No felting now with weary hands,
The shuttles fly to work, and set
The bobbins reeling fast. One touch,
The engine's tamed! It comes to rest.

He stops the machinery.

Maker and master is the Mind
Of man. Maker and master!
Who fights against machinery
Is godlike Reason's enemy!
The Demon Steam is overthrown
By right of numbers, and the power
Pluck'd from the tyrant's throne is made
Obedient to his former subjects!
Once you were slaves to elements
But now their masters, royal masters!
And in Creation's last high hour
The bow of freedom spans the sky
Your arch of promise. Man becomes
The captain of his earth!

JOHN WIBLEY *leaps on to a bench.*

JOHN WIBLEY. You stare like men benumb'd, or turn'd to stone,
      Look on that spawn of hell, and pay no heed
      To Master Understrapper. Have you all forgot
      What Albert said to you?

CHARLES. The engine binds us fast!

GEORGE. It hews our living body into pieces!

EDWARD. We were free men!

WILLIAM. The masters of the loom!

ALBERT. We wove Heaven's flowers into our handiwork!

JOHN WIBLEY. Is this base labour worthy of a man?
   Set clockwork dolls to mind machinery,
   Not Britons!

ENGINEER. 'Tis a fruitless war you wage.
   In all the towns of England and abroad
   Machinery awakes to mighty life.
   It points the forward road that we must march.

JOHN WIBLEY. The man who counsels service to that engine
   Means ill by us! Remember Ure's conditions!

NED LUD. Remember Jimmy too.

JOHN WIBLEY. He counselled patience.
   Patience! The language that all traitors hold!
   We are to sell ourselves for evermore,
   And who dares say to us 'Have patience'?
   What truck have we with State and Parliament?
   We battle with our nearest enemy,
   The engine in the mill. Will you be slaves?

WORKMEN. No!

JOHN WIBLEY. Arms, legs and feet? Or jacks and screws and
   hammers?

WORKMEN. No, no!

ALBERT. We want to work as we were used to do!

JOHN WIBLEY. So we shall gain the mastery for ourselves!

NED LUD. We gave our word to Jimmy.

JOHN WIBLEY. To a traitor!

NED LUD. That is false.

JOHN WIBLEY. Ure's hireling, Henry Cobbett
   Betrayed us first, and Jimmy is his brother.

CRIES. That's true! That's true!

NED LUD. And Jimmy is his brother?

JOHN WIBLEY. Why do you flinch? If you are not with us,
   If you're afraid, then go!

NED LUD.   What, I afraid?

JOHN WIBLEY. Think of your wife!

CHARLES.   Your children!

GEORGE.   Or the devil!

WILLIAM. Think of the Tyrant Steam!

EDWARD.   Our women fight!

CHARLES. They set three thieving bakers on the run!

TOM. While we do naught but prate.

ARTHUR.   What should we do?

JOHN WIBLEY. Now, Lud, a deed to prove that you're our
    friend!

   The old mark offers. Death to the machine!

   A sudden silence falls. NED LUD *goes up to the steam
   engine. The overseer, strikebreakers, women and children
   take flight.*

NED LUD. So Henry Cobbett is his brother?
    Death to the devil's brood – and death!

   *He strikes the engine. The blow falls on the starting lever,
   and the machinery begins to work. The looms are set in
   motion. The workmen shrink back in consternation.*

CHARLES (*crying out*). 'Tis witchcraft! Devilry!

ARTHUR (*after a pause*). I can't speak like John and Jimmy –
    but – but I can take a spade in hand and – and summon up
    my pluck – and mark my man – and – strike! (*He hacks at
    the engine. The flywheel catches him. He cries out.*) Oh,
    mother! Mother!

   The workmen shrink away. Stupor seems to overtake them.

EDWARD. The enemy of mankind has swallowed him!

NED LUD. The enemy of mankind has taken him to itself. (*He
    sees a workman stealing a copper vessel.*) Now give that
    here! No thieving! Would you steal from a dead enemy on
    the field? We are at war, mark that. The laws of war hold
    good. Looters are shot. What are you laughing at? Is it a
    laughing matter when you kill a man in battle? We stand

and gibber at a shadow, brothers. On! (*He rushes at the machine and strikes.*) You hag! You devil-spawn!

The others, shamed into action in spite of their fear, rush upon the engine. It is shattered by their blows.

CRIES. Hey, chain us up, old man of iron! Juggernaut! Break our backs for us!

A storm has arisen.The doors are blown to by a gust of wind, and the lamps are put out. In the gloom is heard an outburst of fitful, crazy laughter.

ENGINEER. Hihuhaha – Hihuhaha!

GEORGE. Almighty God! The engine's *laughing* at us.

ENGINEER. Hihuhaha – Hihuhaha!

CRIES. Run! Run!

ENGINEER. Hihuhaha – Hihuhaha!

CRY. The door! Where is the door!

ENGINEER. Hihuhaha – Hihuhaha!

CRIES. The wind holds it fast! The wind's in league with Satan!

ENGINEER (*on the bridge, as if in a frenzy*). Hihuhaha!
I say to you the engine is not dead!
It lives! It lives! It reaches out a claw
To clutch the hearts of men. Hihuhaha!
Against the villages roll marching hosts,
The fields are wither'd by their sulphurous breath,
And stony wastes are left where children die,
And men are govern'd by a cruel clock
That beats a doleful time – tick-tack, tick-tack
For morning, noon and night – tick-tack, tick-tack.
One shall be arm, another leg, a third
Brain – but the soul, the soul is dead.

ALL.   The soul,
The soul is dead!

A silence.

ENGINEER. Hihuhaha! Hihuhaha!

VOICES. He laughs! He is bewitched!

A CRY. The spirit of the engine has possessed him!

ENGINEER. Hihuhaha! Hihuhaha!
   The greedy jaws of war will gape for men
   And nations will be fodder – brothers foes,
   And justice outlaw'd, order piled in dust!
   Against their Mother Earth her children rise
   To slay her creatures and uproot her woods,
   Her godlike creatures and her godlike woods,
   And shame her motherhood – the end is dust!

JOHN WIBLEY. Grab hold of him! He has the evil eye!
   He is possessed!

ALBERT. Do for him!

CRIES. Strike him dead!

ENGINEER. Strike him dead! Hihuhaha!

Confusion. They try to catch the ENGINEER. *Workmen pursue workmen in the darkness; the* ENGINEER *runs hither and thither. Then voices in quick succession.*

ENGINEER (*in the foreground*). Machine – machine!
   Hihuhaha! Hihuhaha!

CRY. Not me! Spare me!

ENGINEER (*from the background*). I show the way, and I am
      born in blood,
   Hihuhaha, hihuhaha!

CRY. Yonder! Yonder he runs!

CRY. Not me! Spare me!

ENGINEER (*from the bridge*). I am no enemy. No enemy of
      yours!
   Hihuhaha! Hihuhaha!

CRY. He stabbed me!

ENGINEER (*as if from a distance*). For ever crucified –
   hihuhaha!

NED LUD. The Last Day comes!

ENGINEER (*loudly*). Out of the deep I cry!

GEORGE. A man is hanging at the window!

CHARLES. 'Tis the Engineer!

ALBERT. 'Tis Death!

NED LUD. He was possessed – his life fulfilled.

A silence. JIMMY *rushes in.*

JIMMY. You played your brothers false, you perjurers!

CRIES. Scatter his brains! Pluck out his guts!

JIMMY. You broke your oath. Our league was made by
Englishmen. You played it false.

JOHN WIBLEY. Fine words to catch fine birds. Are you the
brother of Ure's overseer?

JIMMY. What does that matter?

JOHN WIBLEY. Answer yes or no!

JIMMY. Yes!

CRIES. Traitor! Traitor!

JOHN WIBLEY. Who mocked our womenfolk – your brother
or a stranger?

JIMMY. My brother – and a stranger.

JOHN WIBLEY. The web is woven.

CRIES. He would have bound us fast to Tyrant Steam! The
devil's drudge!

JIMMY. Let me tell you –

CRIES. Not a word!

NED LUD. I would have staked my head on this man's faith.

JOHN WIBLEY. And would you leave the traitor's tongue, the
traitor's eyes, to live? Pull his tongue from his mouth! Tear
his eyes from their sockets!

NED LUD. Traitor!

He fells JIMMY *with a blow of his fist.* JIMMY *looks at him quietly.* NED LUD *draws back.* JOHN WIBLEY *goes up to* JIMMY *and spits on him.*

JOHN WIBLEY. Take that, if you're thirsty! A stirrup-cup before you start for hell!

JIMMY. Brute! (*He raises himself.*)
I held you for free men, but you were slaves,
All slaves! The masters bought your womenfolk
While you went cap in hand for wages. Slaves!
Cramm'd into uniforms, you cried Hurrah
And stood at the salute. Obedient slaves!
The deed you did to-day is but a deed
Of slaves who mutiny. What do you desire?
The power of your masters – slaves?
The tyranny of your masters – slaves?
The pleasures of your masters – slaves?
The man who flogs you on the road to freedom
Is made your chosen leader – slaves!

A silence.

Brothers, forgive my passion – brother slaves,
There was no man to teach you otherwise.
You fought, but you mistook your enemy.
O brothers, if the working folk of England
Are faithless to their calling, and neglect
To join the workers of the continent,
The workers of the world in fellowship,
To build the house of human brotherhood,
Then you are slaves until the end of time!

JOHN WIBLEY. What, mum! Are you milk-livered, all of you! The tongue from his mouth, the eyes from their sockets!

All except JOHN WIBLEY *rush upon* JIMMY, *and beat him to death.* JOHN WIBLEY *turns away. A silence.*

NED LUD (*going up* to JOHN WIBLEY). John, why were you the one to stand aside?

JOHN WIBLEY. I struck him first and last, behind the neck.

NED LUD. That's false.

JOHN WIBLEY. And are you grieved that he is dead?

NED LUD. I grieve for nothing, since he was a traitor. But 'twas you who shouted 'The tongue from his mouth, his eyes from their sockets!'

JOHN WIBLEY (*trembling*). His eyes! And did you do it?

NED LUD. You were not even looking on!

JOHN WIBLEY. I – I –

NED LUD. Ah, now I understand! You cowardly cur!

He takes JOHN WIBLEY *by the collar end drags him to the body.*

You bellowed 'Strike him dead!' and struck not once!

JOHN WIBLEY. I – can't abide the sight of blood – oh – oh –

NED LUD. What! You would swill blood and can't abide the sight of it! Blood – and blood – and blood – and daren't look on! You cried for murder and would strike no blow. You miserable coward! I could strangle you, but for your slimy neck! What have we done?

BEGGAR (*rushing in*). Jimmy! News for you!

NED LUD. Jimmy is dead.

BEGGAR. You've killed him?

NED LUD. Yes.

BEGGAR. And why?

CHARLES. His brother is Ure's overseer.

BEGGAR. And Jimmy?

NED LUD. His helper.

BEGGAR. Dolts, boobies, clodhoppers! You have killed a man who left mother and brother for your sakes who forsook place and name for your sakes! But whom will you not kill – poor human creatures?

A silence.

GEORGE. Murdered, and none knows why.

WILLIAM. Murdered because a voice cried blood.

EDWARD. Murdered because a voice cried treachery.

NED LUD. Because that man cried treachery! What have we done?

GEORGE. That man?

NED LUD. John Wibley.

GEORGE. Where?

NED LUD. But there – there stood John Wibley – but a moment since –

WILLIAM. He's hopped the twig! He's flown!

NED LUD. What have we done?

GEORGE. He runs to Ure, maybe. He whimpers 'I was not the one to strike the blow.' He plots against us, and betrays his brothers for the thirty silver pieces!

BEGGAR. Thirty pieces – that's as may be. But I know that he betrays you, and he plots with Ure.

NED LUD. What have we done?

BEGGAR. The hour to beat your breasts was earlier, my masters. I came to tell you the police are on the way. One murder is enough. (*Knocking at the door.*) Too late!

VOICE OF THE OFFICER. Give yourselves up! The factory is surrounded!

NED LUD. Imprison us! We know what we have done!
We will pay forfeit for the man we slew!
But after us will come men better school'd,
More faithful, braver, to take up the fight
Against the rightful foe – and they will conquer!
Your Kingdom totters, masters of the world!

The door is opened, and the workmen leave the factory singing their weavers' song defiantly. POLICE are seen outside. For a while the stage is empty, then OLD REAPER and TEDDY enter. OLD REAPER shoulders his stick like a rifle.

OLD REAPER. Is God in sight?

TEDDY. Here's the machine, grandfather.

OLD REAPER. The hour draws near. He is the engine! God is the engine!

TEDDY. Grandfather, here's some one lying on the ground. It's Uncle Jimmy!

OLD REAPER (*taking aim*). Bang!

TEDDY. But look – but look – all torn – all torn!

OLD REAPER (*seeing* JIMMY*'s body*). Hurrah! Hurrah! Hurrah!

TEDDY. Home, grandfather! I'm afraid!

OLD REAPER. No need to be afraid, my children, any more. There is an end to grief. I've shot him – I, a bondsman's son. This evening at the setting of the sun I shot him. There he lies. Our Son, upon the earth, all bruised and broken. Where shall we bury him? In God's acre? To the knackers with him! (*Coming nearer.*) Ah, but how he lies there, how he lies there! And his eyes, his eyes! You poor dear Son of Man! Present arms! Poor dear Son of Man! I have lived to see the day of deeds – and now 'tis past. I'm weary of this life. Ah, poor dear Son! (*He bends weeping over* JIMMY*'s body and kisses it.*) And I will pray the Father, and he shall give you another Comforter, even the Spirit of truth; whom the world cannot receive, because it seeth him not, neither knoweth him. Ah, poor dear Son! We must bury him. We must be good to one another.

The end.

Appendix

Lord Byron's Speech in the House of Lords on the Second Reading of the Frame-Work Bill, 27 February, 1812.

The order of the day for the second reading of this Bill being read,

LORD BYRON rose, and (for the first time) addressed their Lordships as follows:

My Lords, – The subject now submitted to your Lordships for the first time is by no means new to the country. I believe it had occupied the serious thoughts of all descriptions of persons, long before its introduction to the notice of that legislature, whose interference alone could be of real service. As a person in some degree connected with the suffering county, though a stranger not only to this House in general, but to almost every individual whose attention I presume to solicit, I must claim some portion of your Lordships' indulgence, whilst I offer a few observations on a question in which I confess myself deeply interested.

To enter into any detail of the riots would be superfluous: the House is already aware that every outrage short of actual bloodshed has been perpetrated, and that the proprietors of the frames obnoxious to the rioters, and all persons supposed to be connected with them, have been liable to insult and violence. During the short time I recently passed in Nottinghamshire, not twelve hours elapsed without some fresh act of violence and on the day I left the county I was informed that forty frames had been broken the previous evening, as usual, without resistance and without detection.

Such was then the state of that county, and such I have reason to believe it to be at this moment. But whilst these outrages must be admitted to exist to an alarming extent, it cannot be denied that they have arisen from circumstances of the most

unparalleled distress: the perseverance of these miserable
men in their proceedings tends to prove that nothing but
absolute want could have driven a large, and once honest and
industrious, body of the people into the commission of excesses
so hazardous to themselves, their families, and the community.
At the time to which I allude, the town and county were
burdened with large detachments of the military; the police was
in motion, the magistrates assembled; yet all the movements,
civil and military, had led to – nothing. Not a single instance
had occurred of the apprehension of any real delinquent
actually taken in the fact, against whom there existed legal
evidence sufficient for conviction. But the police, however
useless, were by no means idle: several notorious delinquents
had been detected – men, liable to conviction, on the clearest
evidence, of the capital crime of poverty; men, who had been
nefariously guilty of lawfully begetting several children, whom,
thanks to the times! they were unable to maintain. Considerable
injury has been done to the proprietors of the improved frames.
These machines were to them an advantage, inasmuch as they
superseded the necessity of employing a number of workmen,
who were left in consequence to starve. By the adoption of one
species of frame in particular, one man performed the work of
many, and the superfluous labourers were thrown out of
employment. Yet it is to be observed, that the work thus
executed was inferior in quality; not marketable at home, and
merely hurried over with a view to exportation. It was called, in
the cant of the trade, by the name of 'Spider-work.' The
rejected workmen, in the blindness of their ignorance, instead
of rejoicing at these improvements in arts so beneficial to
mankind, conceived themselves to be sacrificed to
improvements in mechanism. In the foolishness of their hearts
they imagined that the maintenance and well-doing of the
industrious poor were objects of greater consequence than the
enrichment of a few individuals by any improvement, in the
implements of trade, which threw the workmen out of
employment, and rendered the labourer unworthy of his hire.
And it must be confessed that although the adoption of the
enlarged machinery in that state of our commerce which the
country once boasted might have been beneficial to the master
without being detrimental to the servant; yet, in the present

situation of our manufactures, rotting in warehouses, without a prospect of exportation, with the demand for work and workmen equally diminished, frames of this description tend materially to aggravate the distress and discontent of the disappointed sufferers. But the real cause of these distresses and consequent disturbances lies deeper. When we are told that these men are leagued together not only for the destruction of their own comfort, but of their very means of subsistence, can we forget that it is the bitter policy, the destructive warfare of the last eighteen years, which had destroyed their comfort, your comfort, all men's comfort? That policy, which, originating with 'great statesmen now no more,' has survived the dead to become a curse on the living, unto the third and fourth generation! These men never destroyed their looms till they were become useless, worse than useless; till they were become actual impediments to their exertions in obtaining their daily bread. Can you, then, wonder that in times like these, when bankruptcy, convicted fraud, and imputed felony are found in a station not far beneath that of your Lordships, the lowest, though once most useful portion of the people, should forget their duty in their distresses, and become only less guilty than one of their representatives? But while the exalted offender can find means to baffle the law, new capital punishments must be devised, new snares of death must be spread for the wretched mechanic, who is famished into guilt. These men were willing to dig, but the spade was in other hands: they were not ashamed to beg, but there was none to relieve them: their own means of subsistence were cut off, all other employments pre-occupied: and their excesses, however to be deplored and condemned, can hardly be subject of surprise.

It has been stated that the persons in the temporary possession of frames connive at their destruction; if this be proved upon inquiry, it were necessary that such material accessories to the crime should be principals in the punishment. But I did hope, that any measure proposed by His Majesty's Government for your Lordships' decision would have had conciliation for its basis; or, if that were hopeless, that some previous inquiry, some deliberation, would have been deemed requisite; not that we should have been called at once, without examination and without cause, to pass sentences by wholesale, and sign death-warrants blindfold. But, admitting that these men had no cause of complaint; that the grievances of them and their employers were alike groundless; that they deserved the worst; what inefficiency, what imbecility has been evinced in the method chosen to reduce them! Why were the military called out to be made a mockery of, if they were to be called out at all? As far as the difference of seasons would permit, they have merely parodied the summer campaign of Major Sturgeon: and, indeed, the whole proceedings, civil and military, seemed on the model of those of the mayor and corporation of Garratt. Such marchings and counter-marchings! – from Nottingham to Bullwell, from Bullwell to Banford, from Banford to Mansfield! And when at length the detachments arrived at their destination, in all 'the pride, pomp, and circumstance of glorious war,' they came just in time to witness the mischief which had been done, and ascertain the escape of the perpetrators, to collect the *spolia opima* in the fragments of broken frames, and return to their quarters amidst the derision of old women, and the hootings of children. Now though in a free country it were to be wished that our military should never be too formidable, at least to ourselves, I cannot see the policy of placing them in situations where they can only be made ridiculous. As the sword is the worst argument that can be used, so should it be the last. In this instance it has been the first; but providentially as yet only in the scabbard. The present measure will, indeed, pluck it from the sheath; yet had proper meetings been held in the earlier stages of these riots, had the grievances of these men and their masters (for they also had their grievances) been fairly. weighed and justly examined, I do think that means might have been devised to restore these workmen to their avocations, and tranquillity to the county. At present the county suffers from the double infliction of an idle military and a starving population. In what state of apathy have we been plunged so long, that now for the first time the House has been officially apprised of these disturbances? All this has been transacting within 130 miles of London; and yet we, 'good easy men, have deemed full sure our greatness was a ripening,' and have sat down to enjoy our foreign triumphs in the midst of domestic calamity. But all the cities you have taken, all the armies which have retreated before your leaders, are but paltry subjects of self-congratulation, if your land divides against itself, and your dragoons and your executioners must be let loose against your fellow-citizens. You call these men a mob, desperate, dangerous, and ignorant; and seem to think that the only way to quiet the *Bellua multorum capitum* is to lop off a few of its superfluous heads. But even a mob may be better reduced to reason by a mixture of conciliation and firmness, than by additional irritation and redoubled penalties. Are we aware of our obligations to a mob? It is the mob that labour in your fields, and serve in your houses – that man your navy – and recruit your army – that have enabled you to defy all the world, and can also defy you when neglect and calamity have driven them to despair! You may call the people a mob; but do not forget that a mob too often speaks the sentiments of the people. And here I must remark, with what alacrity you are accustomed to fly to the succour of your distressed allies, leaving the distressed of your own country to the care of Providence – or – the parish. When the Portuguese suffered under the retreat of the French, every arm was stretched out, every hand was opened, from the rich man's largess to the widow's mite, all was bestowed, to enable them to rebuild their villages and replenish their granaries. At this moment when thousands of misguided but most unfortunate fellow-countrymen are struggling with the extremes of hardships and hunger, as your charity began abroad it should end at home. A much less sum, a tithe of the bounty bestowed on Portugal, even if those men (which I cannot admit without inquiry) could not have been restored to their employments, would have rendered unnecessary the tender mercies of the bayonet and the gibbet. But doubtless our friends have too many foreign claims to admit a prospect of domestic relief; though never did such objects demand it. I have traversed the seat of war in the Peninsula, I have been in some of the most oppressed provinces of Turkey; but never under the most despotic of infidel governments did I behold such squalid wretchedness as I have seen since my return in the very heart of a Christian country. And what are your remedies? After months of inaction, and months of action worse than inactivity, at length comes forth the grand specific, the never-failing nostrum of all state physicians, from the days of Draco to the present time. After

feeling the pulse and shaking the head over the patient,
prescribing the usual course of warm water and bleeding – the
warm water of your mawkish police, and the lancets of your
military – these convulsions must terminate in death, the sure
consummation of the prescriptions of all political Sangrados.
Setting aside the palpable injustice and the certain inefficiency
of the Bill, are there not capital punishments sufficient in your
statutes? Is there not blood enough upon your penal code, that
more must be poured forth to ascend to heaven and testify
against you? How will you carry the Bill into effect? Can you
commit a whole county to their prisons? Will you erect a gibbet
in every field, and hang up men like scarecrows? or will you
proceed (as you must to bring this measure into effect) by
decimation? place the county under martial law? depopulate
and lay waste all around you? and restore Sherwood Forest as
an acceptable gift to the crown, in its former condition of a
royal chase and an asylum for outlaws? Are these the remedies
for a starving and desperate populace? Will the famished
wretch who has braved your bayonets be appalled by your
gibbets? When death is a relief, and the only relief it appears
that you will afford him, will he be dragooned into tranquillity?
Will that which could not be effected by your grenadiers be
accomplished by your executioners? If you proceed by the
forms of law, where is your evidence? Those who have refused
to impeach their accomplices when transportation only was the
punishment, will hardly be tempted to witness against them
when death is the penalty. With all due deference to the noble
lords opposite, I think a little investigation, some previous
inquiry, would induce even them to change their purpose. That
most favourite state measure, so marvellously efficacious in
many and recent instances, temporising, would not be without
its advantages in this. When a proposal is made to emancipate
or relieve, you hesitate, you deliberate for years, you temporise
and tamper with the minds of men; but a death-bill must be
passed offhand, without a thought of the consequences. Sure
I am, from what I have heard, and from what I have seen, that
to pass the Bill under all the existing circumstances, without
inquiry, without deliberation, would only be to add injustice to
irritation, and barbarity to neglect. The framers of such a Bill
must be content to inherit the honours of that Athenian

law-giver whose edicts were said to be written not in ink but in
blood. But suppose it passed; suppose one of these men, as
I have seen them – meagre with famine, sullen with despair,
careless of a life which your L ordships are perhaps about to
value at something less than the price of a stocking-frame; –
suppose this man surrounded by the children for whom he is
unable to procure bread at the hazard of his existence, about to
be torn for ever from a family which he lately supported in
peaceful industry, and which it is not his fault that he can no
longer so support; – suppose this man, and there are ten
thousand such from whom you may select your victims,
dragged into court, to be tried for this new offence, by this new
law, still, there are two things wanting to convict and condemn
him; and these are, in my opinion, twelve butchers for a jury,
and a Jefferies for a judge!